MINI

ENCYCLOPEDIA

BUGS

D0069547

MINI

ENCYCLOPEDIA

BUGS

Miles
Kelly

First published as *Bugs* in 2009 by Miles Kelly Publishing Ltd
Harding's Barn, Bardfield End Green, Thaxted, Essex, CM6 3PX, UK

Copyright © Miles Kelly Publishing Ltd 2009

This edition published in 2015

4 6 8 10 9 7 5 3

Publishing Director Belinda Gallagher
Creative Director Jo Cowan
Series Designer Helen Bracey
Cover Designer Jo Cowan
Volume Designers Stephan Davis, Rocket Design Ltd
Picture Researchers Jennifer Cozens, Ned Miles
Indexer Eleanor Holme
Production Elizabeth Collins, Caroline Kelly
Reprographics Stephan Davis, Anthony Cambray, Jennifer Cozens
Assets Lorraine King
Consultant Clint Twist

ISBN 978-1-78209-445-6

Printed in China

British Library Cataloguing-in-Publication Data
A catalogue record for this book is available from the British Library

Made with paper from a sustainable forest

www.mileskelly.net
info@mileskelly.net

Contents

 Insect world

Ants, bees and wasps

Butterflies and moths

Flies, beetles and bugs

Termites, cockroaches, crickets and grasshoppers

Other insects

Spiders, scorpions and mites

Worms, millipedes and centipedes

Classification

Experts have divided all living things on Earth into different groups and given them special names. Each group shares certain features.

All living creatures are classified into five major kingdoms – animals, plants, fungi, monerans (such as bacteria) and protists.

▼ *The phylum Arthropoda includes insects, spiders and centipedes. Insects were the first creatures on Earth to fly, more than 350 million years ago (mya).*

1 Spiny green nymph	**4** Dragonfly	**7** Pink-winged stick insect	**10** Giant long-horn beetle	**13** Tarantula hawk wasp
2 Tiger swallowtail butterfly	**5** Cricket	**8** Tarantula	**11** Honeybee	
3 Cockchafer beetle	**6** Stag beetle	**9** Millipede	**12** Wood ants	

▶ *Trapped in sticky tree resin millions of years ago, this delicate insect was beautifully preserved as the soft resin turned into hard amber.*

These kingdoms are further divided into phyla (singular phylum). There are around 20 phyla in the animal kingdom. The phylum Arthropoda is the largest in the animal kingdom and includes insects, spiders, crabs and centipedes.

The different phyla are split into smaller groups called classes. Birds, mammals, reptiles and insects all belong to different classes. Insects belong to the class Insecta. Spiders and scorpions belong to the class Arachnida.

There are different orders within each class. For example, ants, bees and wasps belong to the order Hymenoptera within the class Insecta. All hymenopterans have wings and can sting.

The study of insects is known as entomology. Entomologists have divided all the insects discovered so far into 32 orders.

Orders are further sub-divided into families. Lions, tigers and pet cats belong to the family Felidae. Similarly, all ants belong to the family Formicidae.

Families are even further divided into genus and species. Only animals that belong to the same species can mate together to reproduce fertile offspring.

Scientists called taxonomists give scientific names to living things. These names are in Latin and include the genus and species name.

Insect fact file

🦟 **There are between** one and eight million species of insects, compared to just one human species.

🦟 **Insects are successful survivors** for different reasons, such as their powerful exoskeletons, their ability to fly and their minute size.

🦟 **Some insects** can fly for long distances. Certain butterflies migrate thousands of kilometres to avoid bad weather.

🦟 **Cockroaches** have been living on Earth for around 300 million years. Today's cockroaches look very similar to those living hundreds of millions of years ago.

🦟 **Insects** serve as the largest source of food for other animals.

🦟 **Fairyflies** are the smallest insects in the world. They are only 0.2 mm – that is the size of a full stop.

🦟 **People have domesticated** silkworms for so long that these insects do not exist in the wild anymore.

🦟 **Insects are cold-blooded** animals, so their growth and development depends upon how hot or cold the weather is.

🦟 **Scientists have developed 'insect robots'** that copy the agility of real insects. These robots are used to explore dangerous areas, such as minefields and the surface of other planets. Robots are not nearly as agile as real insects, but mimic the way they move.

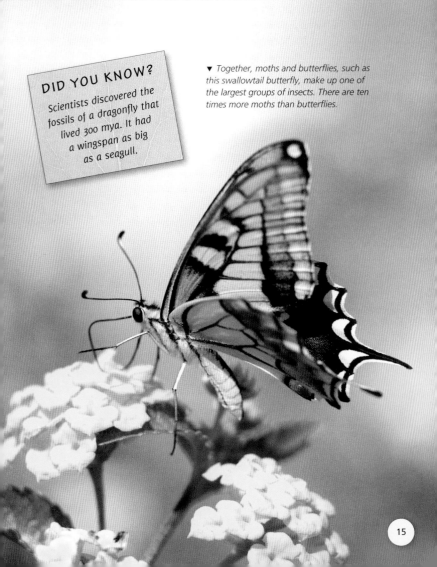

Scientists discovered the fossils of a dragonfly that lived 300 mya. It had a wingspan as big as a seagull.

▼ *Together, moths and butterflies, such as this swallowtail butterfly, make up one of the largest groups of insects. There are ten times more moths than butterflies.*

Record-breaking insects

Mayflies have the shortest lives. As nymphs, they spend two to three years at the bottom of lakes and streams. When they emerge on dry land as adults, they live for an average of one or two days.

Locusts are the most destructive insects. The desert locust is the most damaging of them all. Although they are only 4.5–6 cm long, they can eat their body weight in food every day. One tonne of locusts, a fraction of a swarm, can eat the same amount of food in one day as around 2500 people.

The calling song of the African cicada measures at 106.7 decibels (as loud as a road drill), making it the loudest insect. The male cicada produces loud buzzing sounds by vibrating drumlike membranes on its abdomen.

◄ The giant weta, a type of cricket, can weigh up to 70 g – as much as a small bird!

- **Female Malaysian stick insects** lay eggs measuring 1.3 cm – larger than a peanut! Insects, such as cockroaches, lay egg cases that are larger than this, but they contain about 200 individual eggs.

- **The highest insect jump** measured was 70 cm by the froghopper. When it jumps, the froghopper accelerates at 4000 m/sec and overcomes a G-force of more than 414 times its own body weight.

- **The world's largest known spider** is a male Goliath bird-eating spider, collected by members of the Pablo San Martin Expedition at Rio Cavro, Venezuela in April 1965. It had a legspan of 28 cm – as big as a dinner plate!

- **With a wingspan** of 30 cm, the atlas moth is the biggest recorded moth. It can often be mistaken for a bird.

- **The Mother-of-Pearl** moth caterpillar can travel at 40 cm/sec, the equivalent of 1.6 km/h. It is the only creature that deliberately rolls away when attacked.

- **The larva** of the North American Polyphemus moth eats an amount equal to 86,000 times its own birthweight in the first 56 days of its life. For a human, this would mean an average baby eating 273 tonnes of food.

- **Measuring up to 45 cm**, the large 'human' roundworm infects about one billion people worldwide. Humans can be infected with as many as 20 worms. A female worm produces about 300,000 eggs each day and about eight million in its lifetime.

Insects and people

🦟 **Insects were always** of great importance to human civilizations. People rear insects such as silkworms and honeybees to obtain important materials from them, such as silk, honey and wax.

🦟 **Archaeologists** have discovered prehistoric cave paintings that show scenes of honey collection and the extraction of honey from beehives.

🦟 **Japanese Samurai** warriors painted intricate butterfly patterns on weapons and flags to symbolize nobility.

🦟 **Cicadas and crickets** have been captured and reared by humans for the beautiful sound they can produce. The ancient Chinese regarded cicadas as a symbol of immortality and rebirth.

🦟 **Many insects**, such as mosquitoes, lice and bedbugs, feed on human blood.

🦟 **Some people eat** insects, such as termites, cicadas, leafcutter ants and water bugs, and consider them to be delicacies.

🦟 **Deadly diseases** such as the bubonic plague were transmitted to humans by insects such as fleas, and caused millions of deaths.

🦟 **Doctors** used to insert maggots in wounds to eat dead flesh and disinfect the wounds by killing bacteria.

🦟 **Some insects are pests** and can cause serious damage by destroying crops and fields. However, many insects feed on agricultural pests and help farmers.

▶ *People began to domesticate bees about 3000 years ago. Today, honeybees are kept in beehives containing removable frames. The bees store honey in the upper frames, which the beekeeper removes to harvest the honey.*

Forensic entomology

Insects can help detectives and other experts to solve crimes. There is a special science in which scientists study the insects found on dead bodies. This is called forensic entomology.

A lot of changes take place in the body once a person dies. The corpse becomes host to a variety of insects.

Blowflies are the very first insects that normally infest a corpse. They lay eggs that hatch into maggots. Other insects soon find their way to the corpse, in search of these maggots and flies.

Forensic experts can guess the time of death by studying these insects. They study the life cycle of the flies and determine the time of death. For instance, if an expert finds maggots on the corpse, they can be sure that death occurred a few days previously. This would give the flies enough time to lay eggs and then the eggs to hatch into maggots.

The cause of death can also be detected by studying the insects on the corpse. Sometimes, experts spot maggots and eggs on cuts and wounds in the skin that may have been fatal.

Sometimes, the body is moved from the crime scene. This can disturb the life cycle and normal growth of the insects on the corpse. Forensic experts can detect this change in growth and find out if the body has been moved.

Most insects that live on corpses may be insects that are locally found at the scene of the crime. However, if the body contains insects that do not normally live in that location, the detective can be sure that the crime was committed elsewhere.

🦟 **Experts** can also find out other important clues about the corpse from the insects that live on the body. For example, if someone takes illegal drugs, their body undergoes many changes. These changes can affect the insects living on the body.

🦟 **Flies, beetles and gnats** are some of the most common insects found on corpses. Small spiders and worms can also be spotted on dead bodies.

🦟 **Forensic entomology** is not a new branch of science. Back in the 1300s, the Chinese studied insects to find clues about crimes.

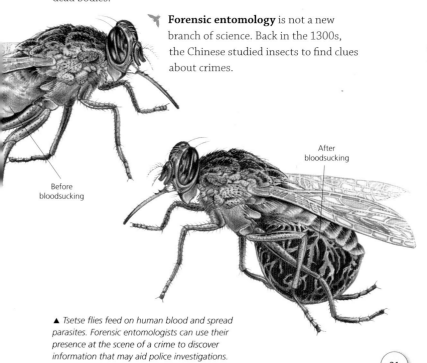

After bloodsucking

Before bloodsucking

▲ *Tsetse flies feed on human blood and spread parasites. Forensic entomologists can use their presence at the scene of a crime to discover information that may aid police investigations.*

Anatomy

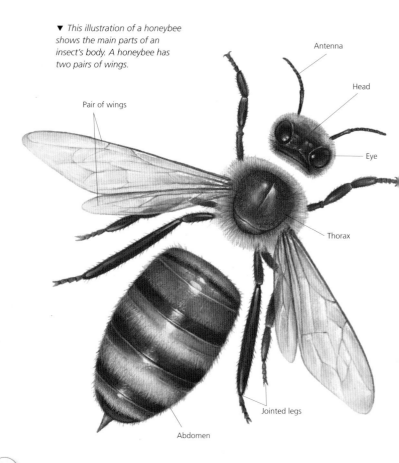

▼ *This illustration of a honeybee shows the main parts of an insect's body. A honeybee has two pairs of wings.*

Antenna

Head

Eye

Pair of wings

Thorax

Jointed legs

Abdomen

- **The segmented body of an insect** is divided into three parts: head, thorax (middle section) and abdomen (rear section).

- **All insects have six legs** that are joined to the thorax. They usually have either one or two pairs of wings, which are also joined to the thorax.

- **Insects have** an exoskeleton, which is a strong outer skeleton. The muscles and delicate organs of insects are enclosed and protected within this exoskeleton.

- **Two antennae** on the insect's head are used to sense smell, touch and sound.

- **The head** also contains mouthparts that are adapted to different feeding methods, such as chewing, biting, stabbing and sucking.

- **Insects' digestive and reproductive** systems are contained in the abdomen.

- **Insects have an open circulatory** system without lots of tubes for carrying blood. The heart of an insect is a simple tube that pumps greenish-yellow blood all over the body.

- **Special openings** on the side of the body called spiracles are used by insects to breathe.

- **Insects have a tiny brain**, which is just a collection of nerve cells fused together. The brain sends signals to control all the other organs in the body.

Moulting

Moulting is the shedding of the hard exoskeleton periodically because it does not stretch as the insect grows bigger. All insects moult during the early stages of their life.

To moult, insects swallow a lot of air or water or use blood pressure to expand their body. The exoskeleton splits and the insect emerges.

> **DID YOU KNOW?**
> A caterpillar grows about 2000 times bigger than its size at the time of its birth. If a 3 kg human baby grew at the same rate, the baby would weigh as much as a bus in a month.

A soft new exoskeleton is exposed when the insect gets rid of its old one. The new exoskeleton is bigger in size and allows the insect to grow.

The new exoskeleton hardens and becomes darker in colour.

Insects normally moult five to ten times in a lifetime, depending on their species.

A silverfish can moult up to 60 times in a lifetime.

The larval stage between moults is known as an instar.

Moulting takes a long time and the insect is vulnerable to predatory attacks during this period. Most insects moult in secluded areas.

▶ *A young adult dragonfly emerges during its final moult. After resting, it will pump blood into its short, crumpled wings to spread them out to their full size.*

Communication

Insects use various methods to communicate with members of the same species, as well as with other animals. They 'tell' each other about new food sources and even communicate their likes (in the case of mating partners) or dislikes (in the case of enemies).

Insects normally use their sense of touch to communicate with each other.

▲ Ants use their antennae and sense of touch as a means of communication.

DID YOU KNOW?

Worker honeybees perform a special 'bee dance' to inform other workers about the source and direction of flower nectar. In 1923, Dr Karl von Frisch decoded the bee language and won the Nobel prize.

Ants release pheromones (special chemical scents) in order to communicate with other ants.

Some insects use distinct colours to let other animals know that they are dangerous. Other insects may have designs on their bodies that warn predators away.

Some cockroaches and butterflies have huge, eyelike motifs on their thorax or wings, which scare predators.

Certain beetles emit strong-smelling substances from their bodies. This is to warn predators to avoid eating them. Most of the time, these strong-smelling bugs taste bad as well.

Strange colours and special scents are not always used to warn enemies. Insects also use colourful displays to attract mates.

Insects were the first animals to use sound as a means of communication. Bees use buzzing sounds to warn about danger, indicate the presence of food and convey various other information.

The rate at which fireflies blink light is very important for successful mating. If a female firefly blinks back too fast, she is thought to be unattractive and if her response is too slow, she is assumed to be uninterested in the male firefly.

▶ Red and black colours, like those on this postman butterfly, are common among poisonous insects. Predators soon learn to avoid eating these poisonous butterflies.

Pollinators

Insects play a major role in the pollination of flowers. In fact, there are many plants that depend on insects for pollination.

Insects visit flowers for pollen and nectar. They are less likely to visit flowers that do not produce sweet nectar. For example, bees rarely visit roses because these flowers do not produce nectar.

Plants adapt their appearance to make them appear attractive to insects. They reward their insect helpers with sugary nectar.

Some flowers smell sweet. This is to attract insects to come close to them. Butterflies and other nectar-sucking insects help in pollinating these flowers by carrying pollen grains on their hairy bodies.

Not all flowers smell nice. Some flowers, such as arum flowers, smell like dead and decaying matter. This is to attract flies and other pollinating insects that lay eggs in rotting matter.

Brightly-coloured flowers attract a lot of insects towards them. Experts have found that butterflies are most attracted to red and purple flowers, while moths are usually attracted to flowers that are pink or white in colour.

Some flowers have strong lines and marks on their petals. These marks can only be seen by insects and are not visible to the human eye. They are like the landing lights at an airport and lead to the centre of the flower where the pollen and nectar are situated.

There are some species of plant in which the colour of the flower changes after an insect has pollinated it. The new colour discourages other insects from visiting the flower.

Insects are sometimes fooled by the appearance of plants. Some plants resemble female insects. Male insects are attracted to these flowers and when they try to mate, the flower is pollinated.

Bees and butterflies are the most common pollinaters of flowers. Beetles also help in pollination, but they are not as effective.

▼ Plants developed flowers in order to attract the insects they needed to carry their pollen from flower to flower. The partnership between insects and flowering plants has helped both groups to survive in increased numbers.

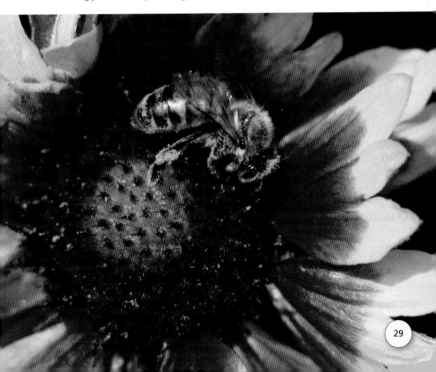

29

Camouflage and mimicry

Hornet moth

Hornet

◀ *The hornet moth is a mimic of a type of wasp known as a hornet that has a painful sting.*

Insects use certain defence strategies, such as camouflage and mimicry, to protect themselves from predators. Killer insects sometimes use the same strategies to catch their prey.

Certain insects cleverly hide themselves by blending in with their surroundings. This is known as camouflage.

Some harmless insects mimic (imitate) harmful insects in appearance and behaviour. This fools predators into leaving them alone.

Hoverflies have yellow-and-black stripes on their bodies, which makes them resemble stinging insects called wasps or hornets. Predators avoid the harmless hoverflies, assuming them to be wasps or hornets.

The larvae of some butterflies resemble bird droppings, or even soil.

Stick insects and praying mantids appear to be the twigs and leaves of plants. Predators often miss out on a possible meal because these insects blend into their environment very well. Even the pupae of some butterflies look like twigs.

Monarch butterflies are bitter-tasting and poisonous, so birds do not eat them. Viceroy butterflies have orange and black wings similar to those of monarch butterflies. Birds avoid viceroy butterflies because they think that they are poisonous as well.

Some moths imitate dangerous wasps and bees in behaviour and sound. Their buzz startles predators, which leave them alone.

Adults and caterpillars of some moths and butterflies have large eyelike spots to scare away predatory birds.

The hornet moth has transparent wings and a yellow-and-black striped body, making it look like a large wasp called a hornet. It even behaves like a hornet when it flies. Predators, such as birds, avoid hornet moths because they look as if they might sting.

▼ *This green leaf insect is almost impossible to tell apart from the real green leaves it is sitting on. Its large, flat abdomen looks like a leaf and even its legs look like broken pieces of leaf.*

Defence

Insects use different strategies apart from camouflage and mimicry to protect themselves from predators.

▼ *This katydid could escape from the formidable claws of a desert scorpion by shedding a leg and flying away.*

- **Some caterpillars** and larvae have special glands that secrete poison when they are attacked. Predatory birds soon learn to avoid them.

- **Stick insects and weevils** are known to 'play dead' when attacked. They simply keep very still and the attacker leaves the insects alone because most predators do not eat dead prey.

- **Ants, bees and wasps** can deliver painful stings to an attacker. These insects pump in venom and cause pain and irritation.

- **Some butterflies**, such as the monarch butterfly, are poisonous and cause the attacking bird to vomit if it eats the butterfly.

- **Certain insects** are able to shed their limbs if an attacker grabs them. This phenomenon is known as autotomy.

- **The bombardier beetle** has special glands at the end of its abdomen, which can spray boiling hot poisonous fluids at an attacker.

- **Some moths**, grasshoppers and mantids suddenly show the bright colours on their hind wings to startle a predator. These are called flash colours.

- **Stink glands** present in some bugs release repelling smells that predators cannot tolerate.

DID YOU KNOW?

When alarmed, ants raise their abdomen. This sends a signal to other ants in the colony, and all the other ants raise their abdomens too.

Parasites

Organisms that live on or in other animals (their hosts) are known as parasites. Insect parasites that live on other insects are often called parasitoids.

Most parasitic insects belong to the orders Diptera and Hymenoptera. These orders include flies, ants, bees and wasps.

DID YOU KNOW?
The eggs of the eucharitid wasp hatch into tiny larvae. These larvae attach themselves to leaves that are carried by worker ants to their nests. The wasp larvae then feed on ants in the nest.

Parasitic insects usually lay eggs in the host animal, which may be many times bigger than the parasite. The eggs hatch and the larvae (maggots are larvae) feed on the host's body.

▼ *Many parasitic worms live in the gut, which is warm, safe from predators and full of semi-digested food.*

1 Flukes
2 Whipworms
3 Pinworms
4 Tapeworm
5 Hookworm

▶ *Gall wasps lay their eggs on leaves. The eggs hatch into larvae, which eat the nutritious tissues within the thickness of the leaf.*

Parasitoids normally live only on specific animals and insects. For instance, blister beetle larvae prefer honeybee eggs.

Parasitic larvae normally eat their way out of the host's body. They may not kill the host immediately.

The most successful parasites are those that do not kill their hosts. This ensures that they have a ready food supply for themselves and the next generation.

Stylop larvae have bristles and are long-legged. Bees pick up the larvae from flowers and take them to their nests. The larvae penetrate the bee larvae and live as parasites, first within the larvae and later in the adult bees.

Parasitic insects are often used to control pest insects. These insect parasites are beneficial to humans.

Some insects, such as lice, live on the human body and feed on blood. They cannot kill us, but lice can cause itching and irritation on the skin. Many of these parasites are carriers of diseases.

Stings

🐝 **Insects that belong** to the Hymenopteran order, such as ants, bees and wasps, are the best known stinging insects.

🐝 **A stinging insect** has special organs that secrete venom (poison) and a sharp sting or teeth to inject venom into the victim.

🐝 **The venom** can have a paralyzing effect on the prey. It can also damage tissues and cause pain. Hornet venom is the most potent.

🐝 **Insect venom** consists of enzymes, proteins and chemicals known as alkaloids.

🐝 **Some insects**, such as mosquitoes, do not sting. They puncture the skin's surface in order to suck up blood. These insects can spread diseases such as malaria.

▲ *A honeybee's jagged sting is a modified egg-laying tool, so only female bees can sting. Male bees do not have the necessary equipment at the end of their abdomen.*

🪰 **Insects sting** for two purposes: to catch prey and to defend themselves from predators.

🪰 **Honeybees sting only once** and die soon after. The jagged sting remains stuck in their victim's skin, which tears out the honeybee's insides.

DID YOU KNOW?

Ant venom glands have evolved to produce a chemical called pheromones, which the ants use to communicate.

🪰 **Wasps sting** their victims many times over because their stings are smooth and can be pulled out of the victims and used again.

▼ Ants normally sting as well as bite. They inject formic acid when they sting.

Flight

Insects fly to escape from danger, to find suitable mates, to hunt for food or to find a new place to lay their eggs. Some insects fly very long distances in search of food, while others cross continents when they migrate.

The wing helps to distinguish between insect groups. In fact, the orders to which most insects belong are named after their wings. The order names usually end with 'ptera', which stands for wings.

Most insects have evolved two pairs of wings, which enable them to fly. The earliest insects had wings that helped them to glide through the air. These wings evolved into sturdier wings that could be flapped up and down.

Not all insects can fly. Some insects, such as female vapourer moths, have lost their wings during the course of evolution.

The size of the wing does not determine how good the insect is at flying. Some insects, such as dobsonflies, have large wings but are poor fliers.

Insect wings are membrane-like structures. They have veins and nerves running across them through which blood and oxygen are circulated. The wing's edge is usually thicker and sturdier than the rest of the wing. This helps the wing to cut through the air during flight.

The wings are attached to the insect's thorax by strong muscles. These muscles help the insect to flap its wings.

In insects such as beetles, the front pair of wings is hard and protects the hind wings, which are more delicate. In flies, the hind wings are reduced to knoblike halteres, which help the insect to balance itself in the air.

A dragonfly flaps its wings as though it were writing the number eight in the air. This movement helps to create air currents near the wings that balance the dragonfly while flying.

Some of the fastest and highest insect fliers belong to the order Lepidoptera – butterflies and moths. This order also has fliers that are the slowest wing-flappers.

▲ Like many other flying insects, the larvae stage of the dragonfly is spent without the benefit of wings. As adults, however, they become skilled and speedy fliers enabling them to catch prey, such as this fly, with ease.

Habitats

Insects have adapted to survive in almost every habitat on Earth, including some with extreme climates.

Entomologists have discovered certain species of insect that live on volcanic lava and others that survive in cold polar regions.

Most insects live in tropical regions where the warm temperatures are most suitable for their growth and development.

Insects can live in the freshwater of ponds, lakes, streams, rivers, and even muddy pools and small waterholes.

Some insect species can live very deep underwater while others need to come to the surface to breathe in air.

Many insects lay their eggs in water and their larvae thrive underwater. These insects fly out to live in the air when they become adults.

Some insects, such as the larvae of house-flies, live on different food materials.

Certain insects can survive on the surface of ponds of crude oil. They feed on other insects that fall into the oil.

Other insects can survive on various man-made food sources, such as glue, paint, clothes and paper. They make their homes in our homes.

▼ *Temperate woodlands are home to a rich variety of insects because of the range of food and shelter available. The numbers and species of insect living in woodlands vary with the seasons and the types of tree.*

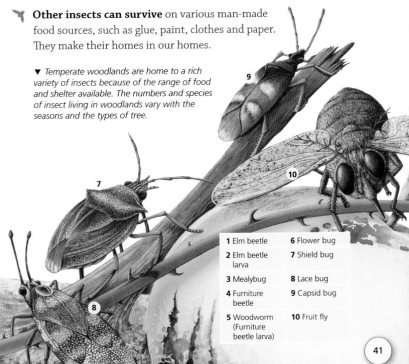

1 Elm beetle	**6** Flower bug
2 Elm beetle larva	**7** Shield bug
3 Mealybug	**8** Lace bug
4 Furniture beetle	**9** Capsid bug
5 Woodworm (Furniture beetle larva)	**10** Fruit fly

41

Migration

Insects migrate across great distances in search of suitable living and breeding conditions. They often migrate when the weather gets colder or hotter or when food becomes scarce.

Migrating insects may land in certain places and lay a large number of eggs before moving on.

Insects migrate in two ways, which are known as homeostatic and dynamic migration.

◀ Migrating locusts grow broader shoulders and longer wings to help them fly fast and for long distances. A swarm of locusts may contain thousands of millions of individuals and fly as much as 3200 km in a year.

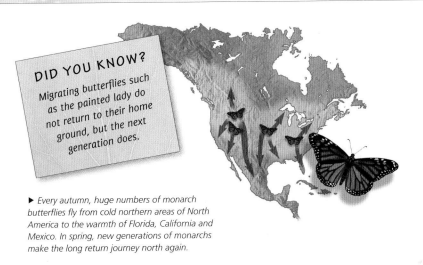

DID YOU KNOW?
Migrating butterflies such as the painted lady do not return to their home ground, but the next generation does.

▶ Every autumn, huge numbers of monarch butterflies fly from cold northern areas of North America to the warmth of Florida, California and Mexico. In spring, new generations of monarchs make the long return journey north again.

Homeostatic migration is when insects pass through a defined path and also return the same way. In dynamic migration, insects depend upon the wind or tides to decide their path of movement.

Monarch butterflies are known to migrate across continents. These butterflies can cover a distance of more than 3000 km.

Butterflies may travel in huge groups of millions of butterflies. Most of the older butterflies cannot withstand the journey and die on the way.

Pilots have spotted migrating butterflies at an altitude of 1200 m.

Locusts migrate across farmlands in large swarms in search of greener pastures.

Army ants do not build permanent nests because they constantly migrate in search of food.

43

Ants, bees and wasps

Ants

- **Ants are one of the most successful insects** on Earth. There are more than 9000 different species.

- **The study of ants** is known as myrmecology. People sometimes rear ants in elaborate ant farms.

- **Ants belong** to an order of insects known as Hymenoptera. Bees and wasps also belong to this group. Entomologists believe that ants evolved from wasps millions of years ago.

- **Ants are social insects**, which live in huge colonies. These colonies consist of the queen ant, female workers and male ants.

- **In ant colonies**, the different ants divide themselves into groups that perform various tasks. Some ants are cleaners, some take care of the young ones while others gather food or defend the nest.

- **When ants find food**, they form a chemical trail of pheromones so that other ants can find their way from the nest to the food.

- **Rare trap-jaw ants** are found in Costa Rica. They have large jaws, which are used to trap and stab the enemy.

DID YOU KNOW?
Birds allow ants to crawl on their bodies and spray them with formic acid. Known as anting, this gets rid of parasites from their feathers.

- **An ant can lift a weight** that is 20 to 50 times more than its own body weight.

- **Slave-maker ants** do not have their own nests. They steal the pupae of other ants and make them slaves in their own colony.

▲ Aphids produce a sugary
substance that ants feed on. In
return, the ants protect the aphids
and 'graze' them in fresh pastures.

Ant facts

Most ants live in anthills that are made of mounds of soil, sand and sticks, but some nest in trees.

Anthills consist of different chambers and tunnels. Each chamber is used for different purposes, such as food storage, nurseries or resting areas.

▼ Ants communicate with the help of their feelers (antennae). They also leave scent trails behind them to let the other ants know exactly where to find the food source.

Not all ants live in anthills. Army ants are nomadic insects. They carry their eggs and young ones along with them while travelling and set up temporary camps.

The largest ant in the colony is the queen ant. When she matures, the queen ant flies off in search of a suitable place to build a new colony.

Queen ants nip off their wings once they find a place to breed. Smaller worker ants also have wings.

Worker ants take good care of the eggs. At night, they carry the eggs into deep nest tunnels to protect them from the cold. In the morning, workers carry the eggs back to the surface to warm them.

Male ants die shortly after mating with the queen ant.

Ants have two stomachs. One stomach carries its own food while the other carries food that will be shared with other ants. This is called the crop.

Each ant colony has a unique smell that helps the members to identify each other. This also helps the ants to detect an intruder in the nest.

Ant nests

Ants live in nests that are built by the worker ants. These nests are known as formicariums.

Ant nests are usually built on the ground. These nests can be either underground or above the soil. Some species of ant support their nests by building them against man-made structures, such as telephone poles.

▼ *Ants can build large and complex nests. This is due to their social lifestyle and great strength – a single ant may lift an object 20 times its own body weight.*

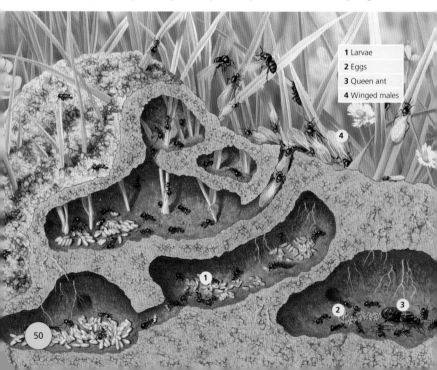

1 Larvae
2 Eggs
3 Queen ant
4 Winged males

- **Ant nests that are built** above the ground are in the form of mounds of soil, twigs and leaves. Some ant mounds can be as tall as one metre. These ant nests are many metres wide.

- **Different species** of ant build different kinds of nests. Some nests are simple with only a few chambers and corridors, while other nests are complex and have separate chambers for the queen, the eggs and the young.

- **Worker ants** take care to control the temperature inside the nest and ensure that there is proper ventilation in the chambers. The walls of these chambers are made smooth with mud and saliva.

- **Some species** of ant grow 'fungus gardens' inside their nests. These gardens provide food for the young ants. There are special cells inside the nest used to store food material for the fungus.

- **Certain ants** build nests in trees. These nests are not confined to a single tree. The ants connect the different trees with the help of underground tunnels and corridors.

- **Leafcutter ants** make the largest ant nests. Some leafcutter nests contain millions of worker ants.

- **Ants sometimes make use** of old, empty wasp nests. They also live in tree galls, dead wood and tree stumps.

DID YOU KNOW?

The pagoda tree ant builds its nest with wood pulp and saliva. These ants place small scraps of tree bark one on top of the other making a tall structure that looks like an oriental pagoda.

Army ant

Army ants constantly migrate in search of food. They can attack and enslave ants living in other colonies. Army ants march at night and stop to camp in the morning.

Nomadic in nature, army ants do not build permanent nests.

Temporary nests are formed by army ants while the queen lays her eggs. The ants cling onto each other and form the walls and chambers.

Army ants are voracious eaters. They march in swarms of up to one million ants and eat almost 50,000 insects a day!

▼ *The army ants of tropical America march in columns, just like real soldiers. To cross gaps, some of the ants form bridges with their bodies, allowing the rest of the army to swarm over the living bridge. The worker ants also link up to form chains that surround the queen and young.*

These ants eat insects, birds and small animals that cross their path. Army ants can even eat a horse.

Army ants have simple eyes, not compound eyes like other ant species. However, worker army ants are blind.

Army ants have not evolved (changed) much in the last 100 million years.

Some people allow army ants to march into their homes and clear them of insects and other pests.

DID YOU KNOW?
A queen army ant can lay up to four million eggs in one month.

53

Leafcutter ant

🐜 **Leafcutter ants** cut out bits of leaves from plants and carry them back to their underground nest.

🐜 **These ants cannot digest leaves**. Leafcutter ants feed on a fungus that is specially grown by them.

🐜 **The cut leaf pieces** are used to fertilize special fungus farms that are grown inside the ant nest. There can be numerous fungus farms in a single nest.

🐜 **Leafcutter ants** are normally found in tropical rainforests.

🐜 **A queen leafcutter ant** can produce about 15 million offspring during her lifetime.

🐜 **Leafcutter ants divide** themselves into workers and soldiers. The biggest ants are soldiers, which protect the nest.

▶ Leafcutter ants carry cut pieces of leaf back to their nest. Each leaf fragment can take two or three minutes to cut and is often many times the size of the ant.

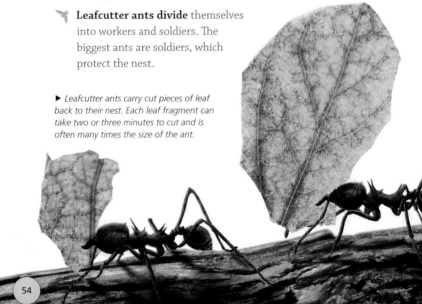

Small worker ants take care of the young and manage the nest, while bigger worker ants go out and cut pieces of leaves for the fungus farms.

In some species of leafcutter ant, tiny workers ride on the pieces of snipped leaves. They protect the larger workers from flies that try to lay their eggs on them.

In some cultures, leafcutter ants are eaten. They are a rich source of protein.

Leafcutter ants do not sting, but they can bite.

Weaver ant

🐜 **Weaver ants** build their colonies in the top of trees, using live green leaves.

🐜 **The larvae of weaver ants** secrete a sticky silklike substance. Adult ants use the young larvae like glue sticks.

🐜 **A team of adult worker weaver ants** holds two leaves together, while a single worker holding a larva runs through the edges and 'sews' them together. The worker ant holds the larva in its mandibles (mouthparts) and uses the silky secretion to stick the leaves together.

🐜 **A colony can contain** about 150 weaver nests in 20 different trees. The queen ant's nest is built in the centre of the colony. It is made with extra silk and is feathery in appearance.

🐜 **The larger worker (soldier) ants** fiercely protect their nest, while the smaller workers take care of various chores inside the nest.

🐜 **Weaver ants are carnivores** and feed on body fluids from small, soft-bodied insects. Some species also feed on honeydew.

🐜 **For 2000 years,** the Chinese have used weaver ants to control pest infestations in their crop fields.

DID YOU KNOW?

Weaver ants are eaten in Eastern cultures. Adult ants have a lemony taste and are used to flavour rice. The pupae are said to be creamy in taste. The oil extracted from these ants is used as a sweetener.

▲ *Weaver ants join leaves together to make their nests.*

Weaver ants do not sting but they can inflict very painful bites if provoked. When they bite, weaver ants squirt formic acid into the wound, causing even more pain.

Some caterpillars and spiders camouflage themselves as weaver ants and attack weaver ant nests. The spiders may even smell like weaver ants.

Bees

🐝 **There are approximately 20,000** species of bee. Many bees live alone but over 500 species are social and live in colonies.

🐝 **Bees are small** in size, ranging from 2–4 cm in length. They have a sting to protect them.

🐝 **Generally black or grey** in colour, bees can also be yellow, red, green or blue.

🐝 **Bees feed on pollen and nectar** collected from flowers. Hairs on their body help them to collect the pollen. Pollen contains protein and nectar provides energy.

🐝 **Social bees secrete wax** to build their nests. A honeybee colony may contain 3000 to 40,000 bees depending on the species, the season and the locality. It consists of a single queen bee, female workers and male drones.

🐝 **Male drones** do not have stings and their function is to mate with the queen bee. The queen lays about 600 to 700 eggs every day.

🐝 **Bees have five eyes**. They have two compound eyes and three simple eyes, or ocelli. Bees can see ultraviolet light, which is invisible to the human eye.

🐝 **A normal bee's lifespan** ranges from five to six weeks but a queen bee can live for up to five years.

🐝 **Bees communicate** with other bees about the distance, direction and quality or quantity of the food source through a unique combination of dance and sounds.

A honeybee attacks either to protect itself or its colony. Once a bee stings, it leaves behind its sting and venom in the victim's body. As the bee pulls away from the victim its organs are pulled out of its abdomen, killing the bee.

▼ *Honeybee workers crowd around their queen. The workers lick and stroke their queen to pick up powerful scents called pheromones, which pass on information about the queen and tell the workers how to behave.*

59

Bee behaviour

🐝 **Bees have two kinds** of mouthparts. The first kind, found in honeybees, is adapted for sucking. The other kind is adapted for biting. This is found in carpenter bees.

🐝 **The antennae** are the organs of touch and smell. Bees use their antennae to detect flower fragrances and to find nectar.

🐝 **Bees can rarely distinguish** sweet and bitter tastes but can identify sour and salty tastes. Bees use their front legs, antennae and proboscis for tasting.

▼ *This bee's long, pink, ridged glossa (tongue) laps up nectar from deep in the flower. Bees are well equipped to eat both solids and liquids, and to fashion wax to make cells for the honeycomb.*

Bees have no sense of hearing, but they can sense vibrations through their sensitive hairs.

Bees do not sleep, although they may remain motionless.

Wild bees nest underground or in tree holes, caves or under houses. Honeybees also live in hives constructed by people.

Social bees follow a hierarchical structure. They live in large colonies of queens, males and workers. The queen's cell is structurally different from the worker cells. Males do not help in the organization and other activities of the colony.

When a colony becomes overcrowded, some bees fly to a different location. This phenomenon is called swarming. It is a part of the annual life cycle of the bee colony.

A division of labour exists among social bees. The queen bee lays eggs and male bees fertilize the queen bee. Worker bees perform various tasks, such as cleaning the cells, keeping the young warm and guarding them, feeding larvae, producing wax and collecting food for the colony.

The queen bee secretes pheromones, which tell worker bees that she is alive and well and also inhibit the development of worker bees into queens. Once she lays eggs, the fertilized eggs become female worker bees and the unfertilized eggs become male bees.

Bee facts

🐝 **Bees belong** to the order Hymenoptera. Ants and wasps also belong to this order.

🐝 **Bees look like wasps** but they have more hair and thicker, more robust, bodies. Unlike wasps, bees have specialized organs to carry pollen.

> **DID YOU KNOW?**
> Bees cannot see the colour red. They are mainly attracted to blue and yellow flowers and visit these flowers more often.

🐝 **The most important group** of pollinating insects is formed by bees. People have used bees since prehistoric times to pollinate crops.

🐝 **Entomologists** distinguish between bee species and families by studying the subtle differences in the veins of their wings, their body structures and their nesting and feeding habits.

🐝 **The richest diversity of bees** is found mostly in the northern regions of Mexico and southern Arizona, USA.

🐝 **Solitary bees do not live** in large colonies and build their own nests where they rear their offspring.

🐝 **Some of the best known** solitary bee species are carpenter bees, leafcutter bees and mason bees.

🐝 **The popular honeybee species**, *Apis mellifera*, is commonly found in Europe, Africa, Asia, the Middle East and the Americas. The scientific name of the honeybee means 'honey carrier'.

Bees are very hardworking insects. The term 'busy as a bee' comes from their tireless way of collecting pollen and nectar from flowers.

Fossil records show that the first bees appeared in the Miocene Epoch some 26,000,000 years ago. These were the leafcutter bees.

▲ Bees are important because they carry pollen from flower to flower so that seeds can grow. The bright colours of flowers and the nectar they produce encourage bees to visit them.

Bee nests

🐝 **Social bees make complex nests,** which consist of a number of cells, often built in flat sheets called combs.

🐝 **Social bees,** such as honeybees, bumblebees and stingless bees, make cells of wax. However, honeybees are the only species that make prominent honeycombs. People sometimes keep honeybees in beehives for their honey.

🐝 **Honeycombs** are made up of hexagonal cells divided into three main sections. The upper section is used for storing honey and the middle section for storing pollen. The lower section is used to house the eggs and young.

🐝 **The hexagonal shape** of the honeycomb cells allows the maximum amount of honey to be stored and uses the least amount of wax.

🐝 **Social bees use their nests** to raise their eggs, larvae and pupae, collectively called their brood. Some also use their nests to prepare and store honey for the winter.

🐝 **Bees use 'bee glue' (propolis),** a sticky tree resin, to strengthen and repair their nests.

🐝 **To maintain an optimum temperature** of 35°C in the beehive, bees use water as a coolant. They also flutter their wings to maintain the temperature at the correct level.

🐝 **Stingless bees build** saclike combs. They are made from a mixture of resin and wax called cerumen. The combs are held together by propolis in the hollows of trees, rocks and walls. While building their nest, stingless bees hang the cells horizontally instead of aligning them vertically, as honeybees do.

A bumblebee queen builds her nest in a hole in the ground. She may use the abandoned nests of birds, mice, ants or termites.

▼ A honeybee hive showing some of the cells used for storing pollen, honey, eggs and developing larvae.

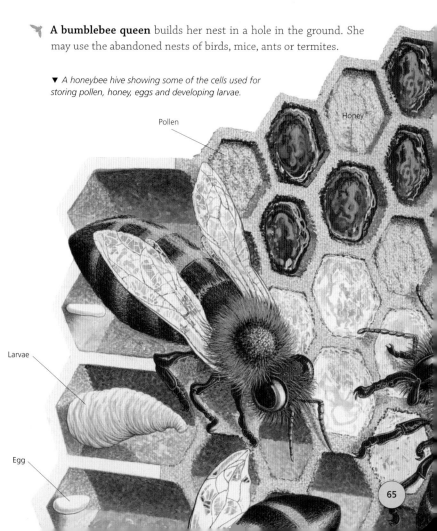

Pollen

Honey

Larvae

Egg

65

Honey

▶ *A natural honeycomb, showing the double layer of six-sided cells constructed by the bees to store honey. The honeycomb is used in the winter as food for the larvae and other members of the bee colony.*

Honey is a natural, unrefined sweetener, which is an alternative to sugar.

Every 100 g of honey provides 319 kilocalories of energy.

Bees collect the nectar of flowers, and other plant secretions, and turn it into honey. It is then altered chemically into different types of sugars and stored in the comb cells.

The honey in a honeycomb includes matured nectar, pollen, bee saliva and wax granules.

Honey mainly contains moisture, sugars and minerals. Trace elements, such as calcium, phosphorous, magnesium, iron, silica and vitamin C, are also present.

Honey is considered to be the only source of food that has all the energy and protein reserves necessary to sustain life.

The colour and flavour of honey depends upon the climate and the flowers from which the nectar has been collected.

Honey serves as an important source of medicines because of its mild laxative, bactericidal, sedative, antiseptic and alkaline characteristics.

Honey extracted from wild beehives can be dangerous if the nectar is obtained from poisonous flowers.

Honey is used in a fluid medium in the preservation of the cornea (layer at the front of the eye).

▶ When they remove the honeycombs from a hive, beekeepers have to wear special clothes and netting over their face to protect their skin from bee stings.

67

Honeybee

- **Honeybees are social insects**. They live in large colonies and are the most popular species of bees.

- **Some well known species** of honeybee are Italian bees, Carniolan (Slovenian) bees, Caucasian bees, German black bees and Africanized honeybees.

- **In a honeybee colony**, different groups of bees carry out different tasks. A colony is made up of a queen bee, female workers and male drones.

▼ *Stored honey keeps worker honeybees and their developing young alive during the long cold winters in temperate areas when other bee colonies die out.*

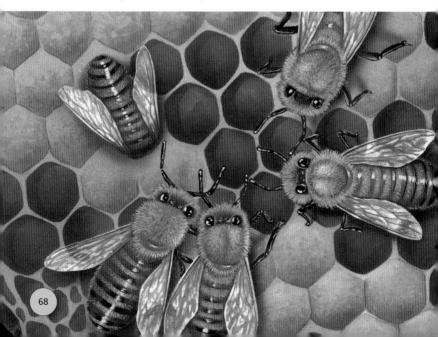

🐝 **Queen bees** are sexually productive and responsible for laying eggs that develop into drones and worker bees.

🐝 **Workers have a sharp sting**, pollen baskets, wax secreting glands and a honey sac for collecting honey. The wax is used to build sheets of cells called combs.

▲ Honeybees have hairs on their body to help them collect pollen.

🐝 **Worker bees build** the nest as well as collect pollen and nectar for food. They are also responsible for maintaining the nursery temperature at 34°C, which is ideal for hatching the eggs and rearing the larvae.

🐝 **Drones do not have a sting**. Their sole function is to mate with the queen. They die after mating. During the winter, they are driven out of the beehive by the workers.

🐝 **The biggest producers of honey** are honeybees. This is why they are the species most domesticated by humans.

🐝 **Honeybees** have an amazing mode of communication among themselves – dancing. Dr Karl Von Frisch won the Nobel Prize for deciphering the bee dance.

🐝 **Honeybees are susceptible** to various diseases and attacks by parasites. Parasite and virus attacks may cause paralysis in bees.

Killer bee

Africanized honeybees are popularly known as killer bees among entomologists and beekeepers. These bees are very aggressive and attack their enemies at the slightest chance. This is how they got their name.

Brazilian scientists first brought the ancestors of Africanized honeybees from Africa to Brazil in the 1950s. These bees were called African honeybees.

Scientists bred these African honeybees with European ones in order to increase the production of honey. The new species of bee was named the Africanized honeybee or killer bee. These bees adapted well to the climate and their population increased rapidly.

Killer bees can nest in natural surroundings, such as hollow trees, as well as man-made surroundings, such as porches, sheds and even garbage containers.

These bees feed on nectar and pollen and make honey from the nectar.

Killer bees can survive on sparse supplies of nectar. Therefore, they produce and store less honey than honeybees.

These bees are known for their frequent swarming. They migrate to new colonies when the climatic conditions are not suitable.

Beekeepers find it very difficult to manage these bees because of their rapid population growth. However, killer bees are useful for crop pollination.

◄ Killer bees are a new breed of bee created by scientists. Killer bees and their less aggressive relative, honeybees, are identical in appearance.

Killer bee colonies can easily become agitated and pose a serious threat to humans and other animals. When a hive of killer bees is disturbed, they can viciously chase their enemies for a considerable distance and the nest can stay disturbed for days. These bees sting their enemies collectively.

71

Bumblebee

Bumblebees are hairy, black, yellow or orange in colour and up to 25 mm long. They are most common in temperate regions and are less aggressive than other bees.

Bumblebees live in small colonies of between 50 to 600 bees.

▼ Bumblebees collect pollen from flowers in pollen baskets (long, stiff bristles) on their back legs. The bee combs the yellow pollen dust from its body and packs it tightly into the pollen baskets until they are full.

DID YOU KNOW?
Bumblebees do not produce large quantities of honey. They store honey just for feeding themselves and their young.

🐝 **Bumblebees build** their nests on the ground in rocky holes, grassy hollows or deserted rodent or bird nests. The chambers are spherical in shape with one exit. The cells inside are capsule shaped.

🐝 **The queen bumblebee** lays her eggs in wax cups inside the nest. The wax is secreted by her abdominal glands.

🐝 **Only the young queen** bumblebees survive the winter. The rest of the bees in the colony die.

🐝 **Bumblebees regulate** their body temperature with the help of their body hair. The queens hibernate in the winter and come out in the spring to lay their eggs and start a new colony.

🐝 **Low fliers**, bumblebees move slowly around the flowers.

🐝 **Bumblebees help** to pollinate plants, such as red clover. Their long tongue enables them to reach deep inside flowers.

🐝 **In summer**, the bumblebee workers fan their wings to cool the developing young. The buzzing sound of fanning is so loud that it can be heard from some distance away.

◄ *There are different species of bumlebee, such as this buff-tailed bumblebee, which is found in Europe.*

73

Cuckoo bee

Bees that are parasitic are popularly known as cuckoo bees.

There are two types of parasitic bees – cleptoparasitic and social parasitic. Cleptoparasitic bees invade the nests of solitary bees, hide their eggs in the brood chambers before the hosts can lay theirs, and then close the chambers. Social parasitic bees target the resident queen and kill her. Then they lay their own eggs in the host's cells, and force the host's workers to raise the young parasitic bees.

Cuckoo bees are found in a variety of habitats, such as gardens and grasslands.

These bees do not forage for food and cannot provide for their young ones because they do not have pollen baskets on their legs. Since they do not collect pollen or rear their young ones, both these roles are carried out by the host bees.

Some cuckoo bees lay their eggs in the nests of bumblebees. Unknowingly, the bumblebees raise the emerging larvae of the cuckoo bees as their own by feeding and taking care of them.

Cuckoo bee larvae have huge jaws and use them to kill the larvae of their hosts.

There are no workers among cuckoo bees. There are only males and females.

Male cuckoo bees help in the mating process and die before the winter starts.

 After mating, the females go into hibernation and sleep throughout the winter, emerging only in the spring to lay their eggs in the host's nest.

 Females have a thick cuticle, which is the outermost layer of the skin. This helps to protect them from attacks by other bees when they try to invade their nests.

▼ *Laying eggs in the nests of other bees may be a successful method of reproduction for cuckoo bees, but it does carry risks because they may be killed by the potential host bees.*

Carpenter bee

Carpenter bees are named after their habit of drilling into wood to build nests.

Blue-black or metallic in colour, carpenter bees resemble large bumblebees.

▼ *A carpenter bee is about 20–25 mm long. It is not as hairy as a bumblebee, with short hairs on its abdomen or sometimes no hair at all.*

- **Carpenter bees are found** all over the world, especially in areas where woody plants flourish. They are common in forested regions of the tropics.

- **Solitary in nature**, carpenter bees do not live in colonies.

DID YOU KNOW?

Adult carpenter bees hibernate during the winter. They remain in their wooden nest, surviving on stored honey and pollen.

- **Male carpenter bees** have white-coloured faces or white markings and females have black-coloured faces.

- **Males do not** have a sting but they do guard the nest. The females have stings but are very docile and do not sting unless in danger.

- **Female carpenter bees** nest in their wooden tunnels. They prefer weathered, unpainted, bare wood. In these tunnels, carpenter bees drill holes, where they lay eggs in individual cells and store enough food for the larvae to grow. There is only a single entrance to each tunnel.

- **People take preventive measures**, such as spraying pesticides, to keep carpenter bees away from their homes and gardens.

Mason bee

🐝 **Mason bees are solitary bees**. A single bee builds its nest and rears its eggs.

🐝 **These bees** are common in the forested regions of the western United States but are found in many parts of the Northern Hemisphere.

🐝 **Although mason bees** are generally smaller than honeybees, some species of mason bee can be slightly larger or of the same size. Male mason bees are smaller than the females but they have longer antennae.

▼ Mason bees lay their eggs after filling the cells with enough pollen and honey for the larvae to feed on.

These bees are not aggressive by nature. They do not sting unless they are disturbed or mishandled.

Mason bees make their nests from the chewed paste of plant fibre or mud. Several species of mason bee build their nests in crevices or holes in wood, which is why they are called 'mason' bees. Once the nests are built, the bees mate in the summer.

A nest has approximately 6–12 cells. Mason bees hibernate during winter and emerge from their nests during spring.

▲ A mason bee builds its nests in wood or in the soft mortar between bricks. While not dangerous to humans, these bees can damage walls and buildings.

People, particularly farmers, cultivate these bees because they pollinate crops and fruit plants.

In orchards, drilled wood is placed to attract mason bees. They are important pollinators of apple and cherry trees, as well as blueberry and other fruit plants.

Leafcutter bee

- **Leafcutter bees** are named after their habit of cutting pieces of leaf to make a protective casing for their eggs. They nest in the soil, hollow plant stems or woody tunnels.

- **Black in colour**, leafcutter bees have hair on their abdomen. This hair helps them collect pollen, unlike other bees, which collect pollen on their legs.

- **Most leafcutter bees** are solitary in nature. Females like to construct individual nests independently. Males are smaller than females and have hairy faces.

- **The female bee** builds her nest using semicircular leaf pieces for the side walls and circular pieces for the ends. Once the cell is ready, she stores pollen and honey inside, lays an egg and closes each cell with a perfectly fitted disk of cut leaf. Then she begins the sequence again until the entire nest is complete.

- **Individual female leafcutter bees** do all the work. They select the nesting place, construct cells, lay the eggs and rear the larvae.

- **Leafcutter bees** are docile in nature with a mild sting. They use the sting to defend themselves from attack.

- **These bees can harm plants** because of their habit of constructing nests with plant leaves. Their favourite plant is the rose plant.

DID YOU KNOW?

The average lifespan of a female leafcutter bee is two months and in this time, she lays 30 to 40 eggs.

Leafcutter bees help some plants, such as alfalfa, with pollination. They do this by carrying the pollen from one plant to another.

Leafcutter bees have many enemies, such as wasps, velvet ants and some species of blister beetle.

▼ A female leafcutter bee rolls up the leaf fragment she has cut with her sharp, scissor-like jaws and carries it between her legs as she flies back to the nest.

81

Wasps

Wasps belong to the Hymenopteran order, as do bees and ants. They have a hard exoskeleton and their body is divided into head, thorax and abdomen. They have four transparent wings and two compound eyes.

Wasps are solitary as well as social insects. Social wasps live in huge colonies while solitary wasps live alone. There are about 17,000 species of wasps, but only about 1500 species are social.

Wasp nests can be simple or complex. Some nests are just burrows in the ground while others are built with mud and twigs and can have many cells and tunnels.

Each nest has at least one queen wasp as well as workers and males.

Not all wasps build nests. Some wasps, such as cuckoo wasps, lay eggs in the nests of other bees and other wasps.

Other species of wasp lay their eggs in stems, leaves, fruits and flowers instead of building nests.

◄ The small nest entrance is easy to defend from other insects and also helps the wasps to control the humidity and temperature inside the nest.

Adult wasps feed on nectar, and fruit and plant sap, while the larvae feed on insects.

Many species of wasp are parasitic in nature, which means that they live part of their lives as parasites inside other insects. The larvae of such wasps feed on other insects and sometimes eat plant tissues.

▲ Wasps have large black compound eyes, which are good at detecting movement. They also have sharp, cutting jaws with jagged edges.

Wasps are helpful for controlling pests, such as caterpillars.

▼ Thousands of wasps live in one nest, built with a papery substance made by the wasps. The queen wasp lays her eggs from which worker wasps hatch. They then help to enlarge the nest.

83

Gall wasp

🐝 **Gall wasps** are small parasitic insects that feed on plants.

🐝 **These insects** are named after their habit of causing the formation of a tumour-like growth in plants, known as galls.

▼ *Female fig wasps lay their eggs on some of the flowers inside immature figs. The eggs develop into larvae, pupae and adults. Adult females emerge and fly off to find other figs in which to lay their eggs. The wingless male wasps die without ever leaving the fig.*

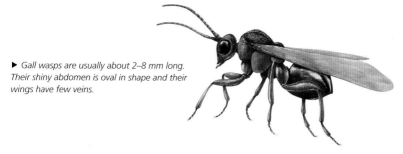

▶ *Gall wasps are usually about 2–8 mm long. Their shiny abdomen is oval in shape and their wings have few veins.*

Galls are an abnormal growth of plant tissues and leaves. Some of them look like greenish apples or berries on leaves.

When a female gall wasp injects her eggs into a plant, galls are formed. When the eggs hatch, the larvae release chemicals, which causes the plant to cover them with soft tissues in the form of a gall.

Galls can be either spongy or hollow inside.

Gall wasp larvae feed on the gall and pupate inside it. Adult gall wasps emerge from the gall either by boring a hole or by bursting through its surface.

Different types of galls, such as leaf, flower, seed and stem galls, are caused by different species of gall wasp.

A gall is like a nursery for one or more species of gall wasp.

Fig wasps, a species of gall wasp, cause the formation of seed galls inside wild figs and in the process, pollinates them. No other insect pollinates wild figs.

Gall wasps are very selective about the plants on which they lay their eggs. For instance, some gall wasps lay their eggs on figs, while others prefer roses.

Hornet

- **Hornets belong** to the order Hymenoptera and the Vespidae family. They have dark brown and yellow stripes all over their body.

- **These insects are known** for their ferocious nature and painful sting. They are huge, robust wasps and are social in nature.

- **Social hornets** form huge colonies that can contain about 25,000 individuals.

- **Hornets can build** their nest anywhere – at a height or even on the ground. They insulate their nests with layers of 'paper'.

▲ The super wasps known as hornets can be up to 30 mm long. Apart from their larger size, hornets can be distinguished from smaller wasps by their deeper yellow colour.

DID YOU KNOW?

Hornets are known to chase their tormentors. Hence the saying 'never stir a hornet's nest'.

- **These insects chew plant fibre** and mix it with saliva to form a papery paste, which they use to build nests. The nest is spherical, with an entrance at the bottom and is divided into many tiers inside. These tiers have hexagonal cells, in which the young are raised.

Hornets build the largest nests of all wasps. A hornet nest can be 122 cm long and 91 cm in circumference.

Hornet colonies die out in one year. No member of the colony survives the winter except the female hornets that have mated.

Abandoned hornet nests provide shelter for other insects during the winter.

Some insects have stripes, which resemble those of hornets. These ward off predators, which mistake harmless insects for hornets.

▼ *Although hornets are very protective of their nest, they are far less likely to sting than smaller wasps. A hornet's nest can be as large as a basketball and is constructed in a hollow tree, under roof eaves, porches and outbuildings.*

Paper wasp

🐝 **Paper wasps are reddish-brown** in colour and have yellow stripes on their body.

🐝 **Social insects**, paper wasps live in small colonies of 20 to 30 insects. After the queen wasp mates, she builds a nest with a material similar to papier mâché (paper pulp). It is made of six-sided cells. The nests are mostly built in the spring.

🐝 **Paper wasps chew** plant fibre, which they mix with their saliva to build their nests.

▼ *This Costa Rican paper wasp is starting to build her nest under a leaf. She will use her antennae to measure the size of the cells.*

▶ *Wasps do not store food in their nest as the cells face downwards and are open at the bottom. The queen wasp glues her eggs inside the cells to stop them falling out.*

Some paper wasp nests look like inverted umbrellas, which is why these insects are also known as 'umbrella wasps'.

A few queen paper wasps build a nest together. The most powerful queen dominates and leads the colony, while the rest become workers.

The subordinate queen wasps are called joiners. Sometimes, a joiner manages to overpower the reigning queen. She becomes the new queen while the original queen becomes a worker.

Unlike other wasps, bees and ants, queen paper wasps closely resemble the worker wasps.

Adult paper wasps feed only on nectar while the young larvae feed on chewed insects.

Sometimes, army ants invade paper wasp nests and destroy the entire colony.

Parasitic wasps

Parasitic wasps lay their eggs inside other wasps, spiders, bees, caterpillars and aphids.

Female parasitic wasps inject their eggs into the body of their host with the help of an ovipositor, or egg-laying tube. Once the eggs hatch, the larvae literally eat their way out of the host.

Parasitic wasps can lay as many as 3000 eggs inside a single host insect.

Some parasitic wasps, such as chalcid and braconid wasps, are known for infesting moth and butterfly caterpillars. They are helpful for controlling the caterpillar populations in crop fields.

Some very tiny wasps specialize in parasitizing insect eggs. These eggs have the ability to multiply into many cells and almost 150 individual wasps of the same sex can hatch from a single egg.

A parasitic wasp can be infested by a smaller parasitic wasp, which in turn can be infested by another wasp. This phenomenon is known as hyperparasitism. This is similar to a large box containing a small box that contains yet another smaller box inside it and so on.

Unlike other social wasps and bees, parasitic wasps do not sting.

◀ The smallest insect, the fairyfly, is an egg parasite wasp. A fairyfly measures only about 0.2 mm.

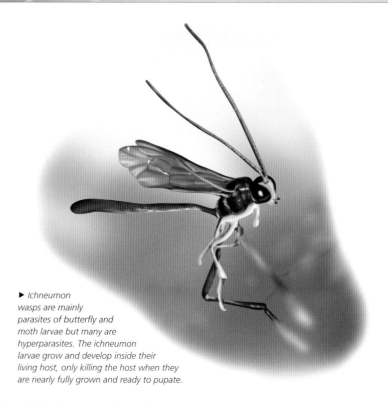

► *Ichneumon wasps are mainly parasites of butterfly and moth larvae but many are hyperparasites. The ichneumon larvae grow and develop inside their living host, only killing the host when they are nearly fully grown and ready to pupate.*

Aphids that serve as hosts for parasitic wasps appear puffy and hard. They die once the wasp larvae are ready to pupate and are known as 'aphid mummies'.

Parasitic wasps are useful to us because their normal hosts are pest insects.

Velvet ant

▼ The tough outer covering of a velvet ant protects it against stings.

- **These wasps** resemble huge hairy ants, which is why they are known as velvet ants.

- **Velvet ants** are usually red, brown or black in colour.

- **Found in dry areas**, velvet ants are densely covered with long hair.

- **When it is too hot** to venture outside, velvet ants burrow underground or climb into plants.

- **Male velvet ants** have wings and cannot sting. Females, on the other hand, do not have wings and can sting. They move about on the ground like ants and their sting can be quite painful.

- **Females** move very swiftly and are often found busily searching for the burrows of solitary bees and wasps.

- **Velvet ants** lay eggs in the nests of bees and other wasps, and are parasitic.

- **The larvae** of the velvet ant emerge before the eggs of the host hatch. They eat the host's eggs as well as its larvae.

- **Velvet ants** make a squeaky noise if they are attacked or captured.

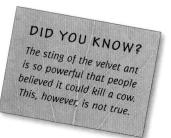

DID YOU KNOW?
The sting of the velvet ant is so powerful that people believed it could kill a cow. This, however, is not true.

Butterflies and moths

🦋 **Butterflies and moths** are part of the order Lepidoptera, which means scaly wings. There may be 200 to 600 tiny scales on every square millimetre of wing.

🦋 **Moths and butterflies** are ancient insects. Fossil records show that moths date back 140 million years and butterflies 40 million years.

🦋 **Butterflies** usually have delicate and slender bodies. Moths tend to have more plump and robust bodies.

🦋 **One feature** that butterflies and moths have in common is that they cannot survive extreme cold weather. Not one single moth or butterfly is found in Antarctica.

🦋 **Both butterflies and moths** feed on nectar as well as on animal fluids.

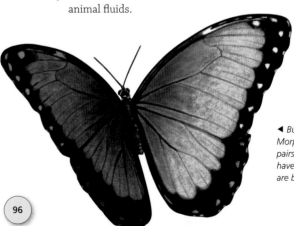

◀ Butterflies, such as this Morpho butterfly, have two pairs of wings, which often have beautiful markings or are brightly coloured.

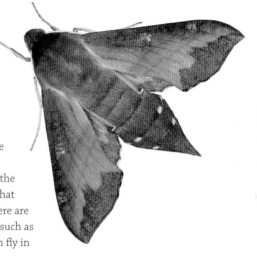

▶ *Moths are more likely than butterflies to be active at night.*

Butterflies and moths are important pollinators of plants.

Butterflies usually fly by day while moths are active after sunset. There are some exceptions, such as the evening brown butterfly that flies at dusk. Similarly, there are brightly-coloured moths, such as the blue tiger moth, which fly in broad daylight.

While resting, most butterflies fold their wings straight up above their backs. Most moths keep their wings spread flat or fold them like a tent over their bodies.

Most moth caterpillars weave a structure around themselves for pupation. This is called a cocoon and is made of silk, leaves or soil. Most butterflies do not weave such cocoons.

The antennae of a butterfly are plain stalks ending in a club (or a hook in the case of skipper butterflies). The antennae of moths have many patterns, ranging from single strands to feathery branches, but they never end in a club.

Butterfly lifestyle

Butterflies do not have a mouth with teeth to chew or break their food into small pieces. Instead they have a long strawlike structure called a proboscis under their head, which helps them suck nectar and other juices.

Butterflies pass through four different stages of development, also called metamorphosis. First, the adult butterfly lays eggs on plants. The egg hatches into a caterpillar or larva. The caterpillar then develops into a pupa or chrysalis. Finally, the pupa matures into a butterfly.

Caterpillars grow 27,000 times bigger than their original size when they first emerge from the eggs. They shed their skin from time to time as it does not expand with their growth. This process is called moulting.

Certain male butterflies have scent pockets on their wings, which disperse pheromones, a chemical that stimulates mating.

Some butterflies migrate in order to avoid bad weather, overcrowding, or to find a new place to live.

The average lifespan of butterflies is 20 to 40 days but some species can survive up to ten months while others last only three to four days.

Butterflies only consume liquid food, such as flower nectar and liquids from rotten fruits or vines. Some feed on liquid animal waste.

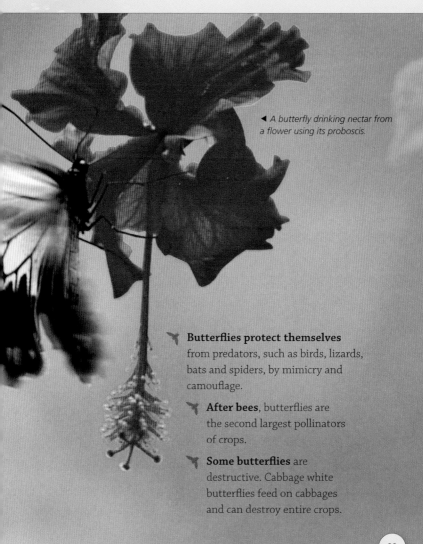

◄ *A butterfly drinking nectar from a flower using its proboscis.*

Butterflies protect themselves from predators, such as birds, lizards, bats and spiders, by mimicry and camouflage.

After bees, butterflies are the second largest pollinators of crops.

Some butterflies are destructive. Cabbage white butterflies feed on cabbages and can destroy entire crops.

99

Tortoiseshell butterfly

Tortoiseshell butterflies are large, brightly coloured butterflies found all over the world. They are one of the most common garden butterflies found in the UK.

Tortoiseshell butterflies can also be found in the dense hill forests of Asia and northern USA.

Adult tortoiseshell butterflies feed on fruit juices or the nectar from flowers, such as daisy and aster.

Female tortoiseshell butterflies are larger than the male butterflies.

After mating, a female tortoiseshell butterfly lays her eggs in batches on young nettle leaves. Each batch contains 60 to 100 eggs.

After about ten days the eggs hatch and the caterpillars spin a web over the nettle's growing tip. Tortoiseshell caterpillars live in groups and feed on the nettle leaves.

Tortoiseshell caterpillars grow to about 2 cm in length within four weeks. Black, with two yellow broken lines along their sides, these caterpillars are poisonous.

🦋 **Tortoiseshell butterfly** pupae are greyish-brown and have metallic spots. These pupae are often seen hanging from posts, walls and tree trunks.

🦋 **Tortoiseshell butterflies** used to be known as the 'devil's butterfly' in Scotland.

▼ *Tortoiseshell butterflies have a long life as adults, surviving for about ten months from one summer to another.*

Red admiral butterfly

The red admiral butterfly is easy to recognize. It is black in colour, with red bands and white markings on the upper and lower wings. Its wingspan is 4.5 to 7.6 cm.

Red admirals are found in gardens, orchards and woodlands across Europe, North America and Asia.

Adult red admiral butterflies feed on flowers and rotting fruits, while caterpillars feed on nettle plants.

This species is known for its migratory behaviour. Red admiral butterflies cannot survive cold winters. Once the winter sets in, they migrate to warmer places.

The red admiral has a very erratic, rapid flight. Unusually for a butterfly, it sometimes flies at night.

◀ Red admirals use their proboscis, a strawlike mouthpart, to suck nectar from flowers such as buddleia.

🪶 **Female red admiral** butterflies lay their eggs on nettle leaves. After seven days, the caterpillar emerges and folds leaves around itself to make a protective tent. The leaves are held together with silk threads and the caterpillar feeds inside its leaf shelter.

🪶 **The caterpillars** are black to greenish-grey in colour and have a yellow line running along each side.

🪶 **Adult red admiral butterflies** may hibernate in winter, storing enough fat in their bodies for survival.

🪶 **Red admiral butterflies feed** on tree sap, rotting fruit and bird droppings. They also feed on the nectar of plants, such as common milkweed, red clover, aster and alfalfa.

▲ *Named after their 'admirable' colours, red admiral butterflies are easily recognized by their dark-coloured wings with red bands and white spots.*

DID YOU KNOW?

Red admiral butterflies prefer moist woods, gardens, parks, marshes and moist fields. During migration, these butterflies can be found in almost any habitat, from the tundra in Canada to subtropical countries near the Equator.

Monarch butterfly

- **Monarch butterflies are found** all over the world, except in cold regions. They are bright black and orange in colour and have a wingspan ranging up to 10 cm.

- **These butterflies use** their body colour to frighten off enemies. The orange colour is considered a warning sign.

- **Monarch caterpillars feed** on milkweed plants, retaining the sap in their bodies even when they mature into butterflies. Birds attempting to eat monarchs dislike the taste and spit them out.

- **Monarchs are beneficial** for crops as they eat milkweed plants, which are weeds.

> **DID YOU KNOW?**
> Monarch butterflies from northern USA and Canada migrate to the Sierra Madre Mountains, west of Mexico City, in the winter. Their location there was first discovered in 1975.

▶ *Monarch caterpillars eat milkweed plants, which are poisonous to predatory birds.*

▶ *Monarch butterflies travel up to 4000 km when they fly south for the winter.*

Monarch caterpillars are brightly coloured, with bold black-and-white stripes.

Male monarch butterflies have dark spots called scent scales on their hind wings. Females do not have scent scales.

A monarch butterfly takes approximately one month to mature from an egg into an adult butterfly. Adult monarch butterflies feed on flower nectar and water.

Long-distance migratory insects, monarch butterflies guide themselves during migration using the position of the Sun and the magnetic field of the Earth.

Habitat destruction and changes caused by logging are constant threats to monarch butterflies. Spraying of pesticides for weed control kills milkweed plants. This endangers the habitat and food source of these butterflies.

Bhutan glory butterfly

- **Bhutan glory butterflies** are found in Bhutan and north-eastern parts of Asia.

- **These butterflies** prefer to live in grass fields and undisturbed forests.

- **The wings** of Bhutan glory butterflies measure about 9–11 cm. They are black in colour.

- **Bhutan glory butterflies breed** twice a year from May to June and then August to October.

- **Very little** is known about the life-history of Bhutan glory butterflies.

- **Bhutan glory butterflies** protect themselves from predators by absorbing poison from the plants they feed on.

- **Experts believe** that these insects probably feed on the poisonous Indian birthwort plant.

- **These butterflies** fly at altitudes of 1700–3000 m in the mountains.

- **In the past** Bhutan glory butterflies were collected in large numbers. Now, their numbers have been greatly reduced and they are very rare.

- **Today, Bhutan glory butterflies** are listed as an endangered and protected species.

DID YOU KNOW?

When at rest, the Bhutan glory butterfly hides its colourful orange back wings with its front wings. This provides camouflage from predators.

▲ *If disturbed, a Bhutan glory butterfly quickly opens and shuts it wings, exposing its bright orange markings. These sudden flashes of colour may confuse a predator and allow the butterfly time to escape.*

Painted lady butterfly

▲ *The painted lady butterfly can be distinguished from the tortoiseshell butterfly by the white marks on the black tips of its front wings.*

- **The painted lady butterfly** is popularly known as the thistle butterfly because its caterpillar primarily feeds on thistle plants. It is also known as cosmopolite because it is found worldwide.

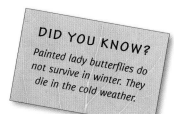

- **The painted lady** is one of the best known butterflies in the world.

- **Painted lady butterflies** are mostly found in temperate regions across Asia, Europe and North America, especially around flowery meadows and fields.

- **These butterflies are primarily** black, brown and orange in colour. They have a wingspan of 4–5 cm.

- **Female painted lady butterflies** lay eggs on plants, such as thistles. After three to five days, they hatch into caterpillars. The caterpillars transform into pupae and finally emerge as colourful butterflies.

- **The caterpillar**, or larva, lives in a silky nest woven around the plant on which it feeds.

- **Adult painted lady butterflies** feed on nectar from flowers, such as aster, cosmos, ironweed and joe-pye weed.

- **An adult** painted lady butterfly lives for only two weeks.

- **Painted lady butterflies are strong fliers** and long-distance migrants. They can travel thousands of kilometres, sometimes with thousands of individuals flying together.

Birdwing butterfly

🦋 **Birdwing butterflies** belong to the swallowtail group of butterflies, which sometimes have tails on their hind wings, like the wings of a swallow.

🦋 **Male birdwing butterflies** are brightly coloured with yellow, pale blue and green markings.

🦋 **Female birdwing butterflies** have cream and chocolate-brown markings on their wings.

🦋 **Predators avoid** birdwing butterflies because they are poisonous and taste bad. Birdwing caterpillars feed on the pipevine plants and absorb poisons from them.

🦋 **A birdwing butterfly** lives for about seven months. These butterflies is listed as an endangered species. People are not allowed to hunt them.

◀ *Queen Alexandra's birdwing butterflies were named in honour of the wife of King Edward VII of England.*

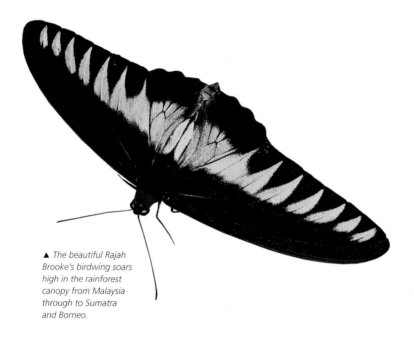

▲ *The beautiful Rajah Brooke's birdwing soars high in the rainforest canopy from Malaysia through to Sumatra and Borneo.*

Birdwing butterflies are found in tropical areas. The best time to spot these butterflies is in the early morning when they collect nectar from flowers.

Female Queen Alexandra's birdwing butterflies are the world's largest butterflies. They have a wingspan of up to 30 cm.

The golden birdwing and southern birdwing are some of the Queen Alexandra's birdwing butterfly's cousins.

Apollo butterfly

Apollo butterflies are mostly found in mountains and hilly regions of Spain, central Europe, southern Scandinavia and Asia. Some Apollo butterflies live above an altitude of 4000 m and rarely descend to lower levels.

▼ *This mountain butterfly has a wingspan of 5–10 cm and a furry body to protect it from the cold. It survives the winter as a tiny caterpillar inside its egg.*

- **These butterflies are cream in colour** with red and yellow eyespots on their wings. They are frail-looking butterflies but are able to survive harsh weather conditions.

DID YOU KNOW?

An adult Apollo butterfly has a lifespan of just one week.

- **Habitat destruction** has made Apollo butterflies extremely rare. They are now an endangered species, protected by law in many countries.

- **The breeding season** of Apollo butterflies lasts from July to August. The female lays hundreds of eggs.

- **Female butterflies** lay round, white eggs either singly or in groups. The eggs usually hatch in August and September.

- **Apollo caterpillars** feed on stonecrop plants. These caterpillars moult five times in their lifetime.

- **Attempts are being made** to save Apollo butterfly populations by means of habitat management measures, reduction of insecticide use and observation of their behaviour during the time they are on the wing.

Peacock butterfly

Peacock butterflies are named after their large, multi-coloured eyespots, which look like the 'eyes' on a real peacock's feathers.

These butterflies inhabit the temperate regions of Europe and Asia. They are very commonly found in lowland England and Wales.

DID YOU KNOW?

Peacock butterflies hibernate to avoid harsh winters. They take refuge in places such as hollow trees, rock crevices or stone walls. If disturbed, they create a hissing sound by rubbing their wings together.

Adult peacock butterflies like orchards, gardens and other places that have lots of flowers. They feed on the flower nectar of thistles, lavender and buddleia and also suck juices from overripe fruits.

Peacock caterpillars feed on nettle plants. They live in groups.

Peacock butterflies have a single brood in a year. Adults hibernate through the winter and emerge in the spring. They die after laying eggs, while the caterpillars hatch out and hibernate as adults.

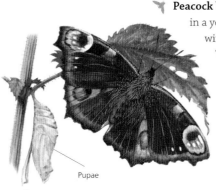

Pupae

◄ Female peacock butterflies often lay their small green eggs on nettles. Adults emerge from the pupae in July.

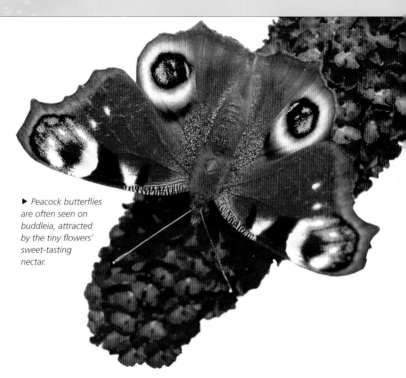

▶ Peacock butterflies are often seen on buddleia, attracted by the tiny flowers' sweet-tasting nectar.

Female peacock butterflies can lay up to 500 eggs. The caterpillars emerge after one to two weeks and all live together in a communal web.

Fully grown caterpillars are about 4 cm long. They have black-and-white spots and long black dorsal spines.

The pupae are greyish-brown or greenish, with metallic gold spots.

Peacock butterflies have quite long lifespans – they can live for as long as one year.

Viceroy butterfly

▲ *1 A Viceroy butterfly splits its chrysalis open by swallowing air, which makes its body expand. 2 It struggles free of its chrysalis. 3 The butterfly emerges and clings to the chrysalis. 4 It hangs from the chrysalis, pumping blood into its wing veins to stiffen and stretch them. 5 After about half an hour the wings are at their full size. Once the wings have dried the butterfly is able to fly.*

Viceroy butterflies are mostly found in the USA, southern Canada and northern Mexico.

🦋 **These butterflies have** black and orange patterns and white spots on their wings – resembling monarch butterflies.

🦋 **They are found** in meadows, marshes, swamps and other wet areas with trees, such as willow, aspen and poplar.

🦋 **There are usually** two or three generations of viceroy butterflies born in each breeding season.

🦋 **Viceroy butterflies** are known to mate in the afternoon. The female butterfly lays her eggs on the tips of poplar and willow leaves.

🦋 **The eggs** hatch and the viceroy caterpillars feed on the leaves. They are voracious eaters and even eat their own shells. The caterpillars are white and olive brown.

🦋 **Adult viceroy** butterflies feed on the liquids from decaying fungi, dung and other animal waste.

🦋 **Predators** often mistake viceroy butterflies for monarch butterflies, and avoid eating them because monarch butterflies taste bad.

5

DID YOU KNOW?
Butterflies practise two kinds of mimicry – Batesian and Mullerian. In Batesian mimicry a harmless species of butterfly mimics a toxic species. In Mullerian mimicry two equally toxic species mimic each other for mutual benefit. Viceroy and monarch butterflies exhibit Batesian mimicry.

Moths

🦋 **Moths make up about 90 percent** of the insects that belong to the order Lepidoptera, which also includes butterflies. Insects that belong to this order have scaly wings.

🦋 **Moths feed on nectar** as well as other plant and animal juices. Some moths do not feed as adults because they do not have mouthparts.

▲ *Boldly patterned, magpie moths have black-and-white wings with yellow bands.*

🦋 **In some species of moth**, the females do not have wings.

🦋 **Most moths are only active** at night but there are some species of moth that remain active during the day.

🦋 **Like butterflies**, some moths, such as hawk-moths, migrate long distances.

🦋 **Some moths** have large spots on their wings. From a distance, these spots resemble the eyes of a fearsome animal and scare away potential predators.

🦋 **Moths are masters** of mimicry and camouflage.

Certain moths can be mistaken for bird droppings when they lie still on the ground. This helps them escape predatory birds.

The larvae of these moths are destructive in nature and feed on different types of natural fabrics, such as wool, cotton, linen and even fur, feathers and hair.

▼ Unlike butterflies, which have clubbed antennae, some moths have feathery antennae.

Atlas moth

Atlas moths belong to the emperor moths group and are known for their large size. They are named after the patterns on their wings, which look like maps.

Atlas moths are the largest moths, with a wingspan of 24–30 cm. When they fly, these insects are often mistaken for birds.

◀ Giant atlas moths have transparent triangles in the middle of each wing where the coloured scales are missing. These shiny patches may confuse predators by reflecting the light.

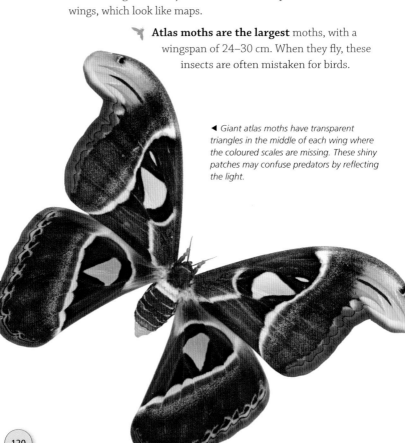

DID YOU KNOW?

Atlas moth cocoons hang from trees like fruits. These cocoons are used to produce a type of silk in Asia, known as Fagara silk.

- **These moths are found** in tropical forests and are natives of South-east Asia.

- **The tips of their wings** are hooked and have patterns on them, which helps to scare predators away. These marks resemble the head of a snake.

- **Males** have large feathery antennae. These antennae are capable of sensing pheromones released by female atlas moths from a distance of several kilometres. Female pheromones attract males for mating.

- **Females are much larger** and heavier than the males. Their antennae are also less hairy.

- **Adults** do not have mouthparts so they cannot eat. They live for just two weeks and die soon after mating.

- **Females lay eggs** under leaves. These eggs hatch into green caterpillars, which feed on leaves.

- **Atlas moth caterpillars** have fleshy projections all over their bodies. These caterpillars can grow up to 12 cm in length.

Death's head hawk moth

Death's head hawk moths belong to the group of moths called sphinx moths. They are found in Africa, Asia and Europe.

This moth is named after a peculiar mark that is visible on its thorax. The mark looks like a skull.

Death's head hawk moths steal honey from bees' nests, which is why they are also known as 'bee robbers'.

At any point in its growth stage, a death's head hawk moth is capable of producing a loud squeaking sound to scare its predators away.

▼ *The caterpillars of death's head hawk moths reach 12.5 cm when fully grown and make a clicking sound if they are disturbed. They feed on potato plants and tomato leaves.*

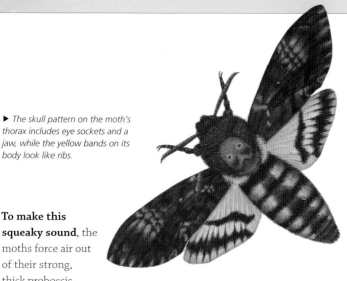

▶ The skull pattern on the moth's thorax includes eye sockets and a jaw, while the yellow bands on its body look like ribs.

To make this squeaky sound, the moths force air out of their strong, thick proboscis.

Females lay single eggs on different plants. They prefer to lay their eggs on potato and brinjal plants.

The caterpillars have a horn on their tail end and are also known as hornworms.

To pupate, the caterpillars make a mud cell deep in the soil and smooth it by pushing their head against the wall of the cell.

Death's head hawk moths find it difficult to survive harsh winters and migrate to warmer places.

DID YOU KNOW?

The strange mark on the thorax of the death's head hawk moth has given rise to many superstitions. In ancient times the presence of this moth was considered to be a sign of death.

Gypsy moth

- **Gypsy moths** are so called because they can travel long distances in a short time.

- **Female gypsy moths** have cream-coloured wings and cannot fly. Males are dark in colour. Females produce chemical pheromones to attract males.

- **After mating**, the female lays her eggs in clusters and covers them with body hair to protect them.

- **These eggs** hatch into larvae, which feed on the leaves of different trees. They wriggle up a tree and spin silk threads. The larvae then swing from the silk thread and allow the wind to carry them away.

- **When the larvae** land in a new feeding ground, they repeat this swinging activity. Older larvae do not swing from silk threads. They feed on leaves during the night and rest during the day.

- **The larvae** spin a cocoon and pupate. Male larvae pupate earlier than female larvae and are smaller.

- **Gypsy moth** larvae are considered to be pests because they feed on the leaves of various trees, such as oak, maple and elm. They also feed on shrubs and other plants. Adult gypsy moths do not feed at all.

- **Trees that** are affected by gypsy moths become leafless. Badly affected trees dry up and die.

- **Wasps** and house-flies often attack gypsy moth larvae when they are resting on plants and trees. Birds and small animals, such as squirrels and mice, also eat these moths.

- **Gypsy moths** are found in Europe, Asia and the United States.

▼ A gypsy moth caterpillar. Gypsy moths were introduced into the United States in the 1860s, in order to develop a silkworm industry. The moths quickly established themselves in the wild and became a major pest.

Swallowtail moth

▼ *This large swallowtail moth has broad wings, like a butterfly, but flies rapidly. In June and July it is widespread in Europe and parts of Asia, often flying around lights.*

- **Swallowtail moths** belong to the family Geometridae of the order Lepidoptera.

- **These moths are** strikingly unusual and can be mistaken for butterflies. They have slender bodies, thin legs and a short proboscis.

DID YOU KNOW?
The swallowtail moth's name derives from a resemblance to swallowtail butterflies. Their hindwings have a tail similar to that of swallowtail butterflies.

- **Swallowtail moths are colourful** and sometimes fly in the day.

- **These moths** are mainly found in tropical countries.

- **Brilliantly coloured species** are very large in size. Their colours are structural and do not contain pigments.

- **Some of the nocturnal species** have eyespots at the tip of their short pointed hind wings.

  - **The eyespots** give an impression of a false head at the rear side of the moth, which protects it from predators. Therefore, during the day, the moths always rest on the upper side of leaves.

    - **The size and marks** on the bodies differ in males and females.

    - **Not much is known** about the life history of swallowtail moths.

Hummingbird hawk moth

- **Found all over the world**, hummingbird hawk moths belong to the hawk moth group.

- **Unlike other hawk moths**, these moths fly during the day and can be easily spotted hovering over flowers in gardens and parks.

- **Hummingbird hawk moths** are brownish in colour. They have black-and-white spots all over their body and their hind wings are orange.

- **These moths** have tufts of hair at the tip of their abdomen.

- **Like other butterflies and moths**, hummingbird hawk moths have long, tubelike mouthparts that are coiled and tucked under their head. They use their long tongue to collect nectar from flowers.

- **Hummingbird hawk moth caterpillars** are slender and colourful. Their horned tail gives them a fearsome look.

- **The moth pupates** in leaf litter (dead leaves, bits of bark, and other dead plant matter lying on the ground) and weaves a very thick cocoon.

- **People often mistake** this moth for a hummingbird because it hovers over flowers and sucks nectar from them, like a hummingbird.

- **Hummingbird hawk moths** hibernate in winter to survive the cold weather.

▲ *The broad body of this hummingbird hawk moth shows that it is a powerful flier. It holds its body still while hovering in front of flowers, beating its wings so fast that they are almost invisible. The rapidly beating wings produce a high-pitched hum, like the wings of a hummingbird.*

Lobster moth

🗡 **Lobster moths belong** to the group of moths known as prominent moths.

🗡 **These moths** are commonly found in deciduous forests in Europe and Asia.

🗡 **The wingspan** of lobster moths is about 5.5–7 cm.

🗡 **Males** are often attracted towards the light, but females do not behave in the same way.

🗡 **These moths** appear in two colour forms – one with light front wings and one with dark front wings.

🗡 **Lobster moths move** in a way that resembles the movements of ants.

🗡 **The unusual shape** of lobster moth caterpillars often confuses their predators and scares them away.

🗡 **As an act of defence**, the caterpillar curls back its large head and raises its legs in the air to startle small birds.

🗡 **The caterpillar** constructs a silken cocoon and pupates in it.

▼ A lobster moth caterpillar confuses predators by suddenly changing shape. It raises its head and tail over its body (making it look like a tiny lobster) and waves a pair of filaments at the end of its abdomen. Lobster moth caterpillars can also squirt formic acid over their predators.

Peppered moth

▶ The dark-coloured form of the peppered moth is less common today in industrial areas where pollution controls have cleaned up the air. The dark colour does not provide effective camouflage against clean tree trunks, which are often covered by pale-coloured lichens.

🐦 **Peppered moths** belong to a group of moths known as geometrid moths.

🐦 **These moths** are delicate insects and have long legs and a slender body.

🐦 **Peppered moth caterpillars** do not have any legs in the middle of their body. They hold onto branches with their first two pairs of specialized limbs called prolegs and a clasper at their tail end.

🐦 **Male peppered moths** have feathery antennae, while females have hairlike antennae. The antennae of male peppered moths are also longer than those of females.

> **DID YOU KNOW?**
> Peppered moth caterpillars are known as inchworms because they move their bodies in a looping fashion as though they are measuring the earth.

- **Males are smaller** and more slender in comparison with the larger and heavier female peppered moths.

- **Peppered moths are nocturnal** and usually rest on lichen-covered trees during the day.

- **Peppered moth caterpillars** camouflage themselves by resembling a twig.

- **There are two varieties** of peppered moths; a paler coloured variety, speckled with salt and pepper (black-and-white) marks while the other is coal-black in colour.

- **During the Industrial Revolution**, the bark of many trees became blackish-grey in colour due to air pollution. Dark-coloured peppered moths blended with this polluted environment and matched the colour of the tree bark. Paler coloured peppered moths stood out as easy targets for birds and other hungry predators, so more dark-coloured moths survived.

◀ *The pale-coloured form of the peppered moth shows up better against dark backgrounds, making it more likely to be spotted by birds and other predators.*

Moon moth

- **Moon moths belong** to the group known as emperor moths. They are found all over the world, but are mostly seen in tropical countries.

- **These moths** have a white body and maroon legs. Their wings are bright green in colour. The colour of female moon moths is brighter than that of the males.

- **Moon moths have a wingspan** of about 10–13 cm and their tail is almost 8 cm long.

- **The hind wings** of males are longer than those of the females. In overall size, male moon moths are much smaller than females.

- **Adult moon moths** have no mouthparts and do not eat anything. They do not live for more than a week.

- **Moon moths** make their cocoons in leaves. The silk of the cocoon does not shine and is brown in colour. This silk is not used commercially.

- **An adult female** lays about 250 eggs at a time, on walnut leaves. The eggs resemble seeds with grey specks on them.

- **Moon moths** grow only at the larval stage. If the larva grows into a small-sized moth, the moth does not grow further in size.

- **Moon moth caterpillars** are bright apple green in colour and are beautifully segmented, with some white hairs.

DID YOU KNOW?

Moon moths are also called 'lunar moths' because of marks on their wings that look like a new moon.

▲ Moon moths have a long tail, which is mainly for show, to attract a partner. By day, as the moth rests, the tail looks like old leaves.

Horse fly

- **Horse flies** are strong-bodied flies with colourful patterns on their bodies.

- **Female horse flies suck and feed** on the blood of humans and animals. These insects get their names, such as deer flies or moose flies, depending on the animal they feed on.

- **There are about 25,000 species** of horse fly in the world.

- **Horse flies** have compound eyes, which are very prominent and occupy the entire surface of the head in the males.

▼ *Horse flies are among the fastest flying insects, reaching maximum speeds of 39 km/h. Unlike most other flies, their flight can be silent, allowing females to sneak up on their prey.*

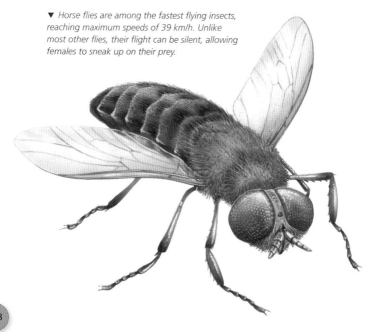

Colourful patterns on the compound eyes are caused by the refraction of light. There are no pigments present in the eyes and as a result, the colour is not retained when these insects die.

The mouthparts of these insects consist of a short, powerful piercing organ capable of penetrating tough skin. If undisturbed, horse flies can suck blood from their host for as long as half an hour.

Female horse flies bite animals to suck blood before they reproduce. However, male horse flies do not bite. They feed mainly on flower nectar and plant sap.

After mating, females lay their eggs on plant and rock edges near water. The eggs are creamy white in colour.

Horse fly larvae feed on soft-bodied insects and other small animals. They can become cannibalistic if there is a lack of food.

While biting and sucking blood from animals, female horse flies can transmit diseases such as anthrax.

▶ This horse is wearing a protective fly cover to prevent flies from biting it and possibly transmitting diseases.

139

Crane fly

- **Crane flies** belong to the order Diptera and are closely related to mosquitoes.

- **Their legs** are weakly attached to their body and often break off.

- **Some of the larger species** of crane fly, such as phantom crane flies, have legs that are as long as 2.5 cm.

- **Crane flies** have extremely narrow wings. They have a thin body with long legs and resemble large mosquitoes. These insects cannot bite.

- **Crane flies are nocturnal insects** and remain inactive in the day.

- **Females** lay their eggs in moist soil. The eggs hatch into larvae, which are greyish to pale brown in colour.

- **The larvae** of crane flies feed on dead and decaying matter. Some species also feed on small insects and others eat plant roots.

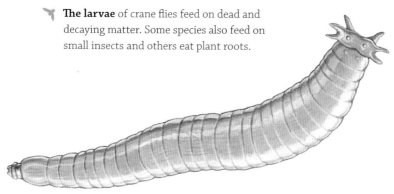

▲ *Crane fly larvae eat the roots of grasses, including cereal crops such as wheat.*

▲ *The long, thin legs of a crane fly are usually twice the length of its body. These insects can also be recognized by the V-shaped groove on the top of their thorax.*

Crane fly larvae are also known as leatherjackets because of their tough, brown skin. They are often used as fishing bait.

Farmers dislike the larvae of these insects because they damage the roots and turf of grain fields and grass crops.

A rare species of crane fly does not have wings. They are found in Hawaii.

Dobsonfly

- **Dobsonflies** belong to the order Neuroptera. They look like dragonflies.

- **Adults** have veins on their wings, which are grey in colour. They are nocturnal insects.

- **Male dobsonflies** have mandibles (mouthparts) that are almost half the size of their bodies. These look like the long tusks of an elephant. Even though these insects look ferocious, they are quite harmless.

- **Females** have small, stout mandibles, which they use to defend themselves. They can inflict painful bites.

- **These mandibles** are not used for eating. In fact, adults do not eat anything. The male uses his mandibles to hold the female while mating.

- **After mating**, the female lays her eggs on tree branches and plants or on rocks near streams. The eggs look like bird droppings because they have a white coating.

- **The eggs hatch** and the larvae drop into the stream. The larvae are known as hellgrammites. They have gills and are dull in colour.

- **Found under rocks** in streams, the larvae feed on other larvae and insects in the stream.

- **The larvae crawl** out of water and pupate near the shore. The pupae are found near the water, under logs or in the soil.

- **Not usually** harmful to humans, the larvae only bite if disturbed. They are also used as fishing bait.

▶ *Female dobsonflies have much smaller mandibles than males but their bite can be more painful.*

House-fly

House-flies belong to the order Diptera and are one of the most common insects.

Like all flies, house-flies have small projections below their front wings known as halteres, which help them to fly. Halteres are modified hind wings, which are used for landing and balancing.

◄ House-flies dribble saliva onto food. Powerful chemicals in the saliva break down the starch and other nutrients. They then dab up the liquid food with sponge-like mouthparts.

▶ *Common house-flies are normally found wherever there is human activity. They thrive on the waste materials left behind by humans and other animals.*

House-flies feed on liquid food and do not bite animals and other insects. The mouthparts of a house-fly are like a sponge, which absorbs liquid food.

Before eating, house-flies often vomit some portion of their last feed on top of new food particles. This makes the new food material easier to digest.

Most of the time, house-flies do not eat all the food and leave some particles behind. These remaining food particles can spread a variety of diseases.

Sticky pads and sharp claws enable house-flies to walk upside down with ease. Fine hairs on the tip of a house-fly's legs enable it to 'taste' liquids.

House-flies have compound eyes and 4000 individual lenses form each eye. These insects cannot see the colour red.

Female house-flies can lay around 600 to 1000 eggs in a lifetime. However, most offspring do not survive to reproduce.

DID YOU KNOW?

House-flies are known to spread 40 serious diseases. A single fly harbours as many as 33 million infectious organisms inside its intestines and 500 million on its body surface and legs.

145

Robber fly

🦟 **Robber flies** belong to the family Asilidae. They are also known as assassin flies.

🦟 **These insects** are reddish brown and have hair all over their body. Most species of robber fly have a long abdomen.

🦟 **Mostly found** in countries with a warm climate, these insects are normally active on warm and sunny days. Certain species of robber fly are also found in dense vegetation.

▲ *Giant robber flies are up to 4 cm in length and are found in North America.*

🦟 **Some robber flies** mimic bees to escape from predators. They are stouter than bees and their abdomen is not as elongated.

🦟 **Predatory insects**, robber flies are fast fliers. They hunt while flying and can attack insects that are much larger and stronger than they are.

🦟 **Robber flies attack insects** such as butterflies, dragonflies, bees and wasps. They hold their prey with their front limbs and then inject saliva into it. This saliva paralyzes and partly digests the victim.

DID YOU KNOW?

After mating, the female robber fly scatters her eggs on the ground. Some species also lay eggs in plants. These eggs are long in shape, while the eggs laid on the ground are round.

🦟 **The body fluids** of the prey are sucked out. Robber flies can only digest fluids, so their mouthparts are suitable for piercing and for sucking liquids.

🦟 **Male robber flies** sometimes perform a dance ritual before mating, which includes hovering in front of the female.

🦟 **Eggs hatch** into larvae that live in soil and rotting wood. Some experts say that robber fly larvae are herbivores while some suggest these larvae also feed on other insects.

▼ Huge compound eyes provide the robber fly with the excellent vision it needs to be an effective predator. Long bristles on the face help to protect the robber fly's face when it attacks its prey.

Mosquito

Mosquitoes are the only flies of the order Diptera that have scaly wings.

Most female mosquitoes have to feed on the blood of other animals to reproduce. They need the protein extracted from blood for the development of their eggs.

These eggs float on water and hatch to produce aquatic larvae known as wrigglers.

The larvae cannot breathe underwater and 'hang' from the water's surface to take in air.

Mosquito larvae pupate in water. The pupa is not completely immobile. It can change position according to the light and wind conditions in its environment.

Adult male mosquitoes feed on nectar and other plant fluids. Only female mosquitoes feed on blood.

🦟 **Male mosquitoes** cannot bite. Their mouthparts are modified for sucking only.

🦟 **Mosquitoes** have infrared vision. They can sense the warmth of other insects and animals.

🦟 **Dragonflies feed** on mosquitoes and are also known as mosquito hawks. Dragonfly nymphs also feed on mosquito larvae.

🦟 **Mosquitoes are known** to spread many infectious diseases, such as yellow fever and dengue fever. The female Anopheles mosquito spreads malaria.

◄ Mosquitoes have long mouthparts that they use to pierce skin (human or animal) and suck up blood.

Firefly

🦟 **Fireflies are not flies** but a type of beetle. These insects are also known as lightning bugs.

🦟 **These insects can grow** up to 2.5 cm in length and live for three to four months. Females live longer than males.

🦟 **Fireflies** have a special organ under their stomach, which emits flashes of green or yellow light.

🦟 **This light** is known as 'cold light'. The process of producing light is also known as bioluminescence. No other insect can produce light from their own bodies.

🦟 **Fireflies emit** only light energy. A normal light bulb emits only 10 percent of its energy as light. The remaining 90 percent is emitted as heat energy. Fireflies do not emit any heat energy.

◀ A pair of fireflies mating on a leaf.

- **Males and females** emit light to attract mates.

- **Fireflies are nocturnal** insects. They live on plants and trees during the day and are active at night.

- **Females** and their larvae are carnivorous and feed on snails, slugs and worms. Most males don't eat but some may feed on pollen and nectar.

- **Some females are wingless** and are also known as glow-worms.

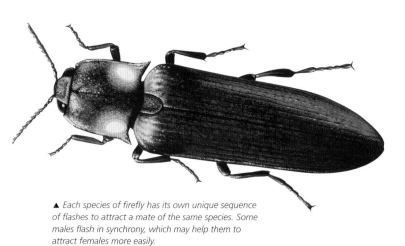

▲ Each species of firefly has its own unique sequence of flashes to attract a mate of the same species. Some males flash in synchrony, which may help them to attract females more easily.

151

Goliath beetle

- **One of the largest** and heaviest insects in the world is the Goliath beetle. Males are as heavy as an apple.

- **Goliath beetles grow** up to 12 cm and weigh about 115 g.

- **Found in many colours**, most Goliath beetles have black-and-white markings on their wings.

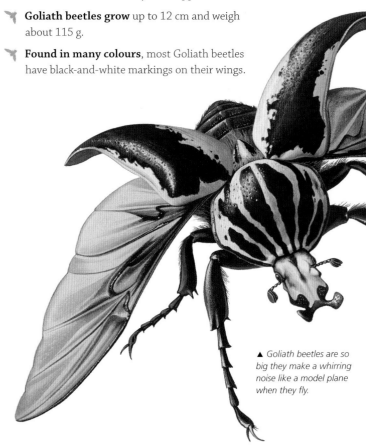

▲ Goliath beetles are so big they make a whirring noise like a model plane when they fly.

Goliath beetles used to be found only in Africa. Today, however, these insects can be found in almost all parts of the world.

Males have a horn-shaped structure on their heads. They often fight each other with their horns.

Goliath beetles are good fliers. They produce a low, helicopter-like whir while flying.

By feeding on dead plant and animal tissues, Goliath beetles help to keep the environment clean.

A fossil of the oldest Goliath beetle is almost 300 million years old.

Scientists believe that Goliath beetles, like some other insects, were much larger in prehistoric times. This may be because there was more oxygen in the air then.

DID YOU KNOW?
The Goliath beetle is named after the Biblical giant, Goliath.

Diving beetle

Diving beetles have oval bodies, which are brown or black in colour. Their wings are shiny and look metallic green when light reflects off the body. These beetles are commonly found in ponds and other still water.

A diving beetle has strong, hairy legs, which it uses like the oars of a rowing boat to push its body forwards when swimming.

These insects cannot breathe underwater and have to come to the surface to breathe. They store air under their wing covers.

Diving beetles often fly at night in search of new ponds.

These beetles locate new ponds with the help of the light that reflects from water surfaces. They often get confused with light that is reflected from a glass surface and mistake it for water.

The **female diving beetle** is much bigger than the male.

Females make small slits in plant stems and lay their eggs inside.

The larvae float on the surface of the pond and move to the shore to pupate.

The larvae are known as 'water tigers' because they can attack and bite other insects. They even eat tadpoles and small fish.

◄ Diving beetles feed on other water insects, small fish and tadpoles.

155

Tiger beetle

Tiger beetles are usually shiny metallic colours, such as green, brown, black and purple. They often have stripes like tigers.

The smallest tiger beetles live in Borneo and measure up to 6 mm. The largest tiger beetles live in Africa and can reach up to 44 mm in length.

Tiger beetles are found in sunny, sandy areas and are active during the day. However, there are some species that come out at night.

Tiger beetles are good fliers and fly in a zigzag pattern if a predator approaches them. They are also very fast runners.

▼ *Tiger beetles have huge eyes. They use their massive biting jaws to catch and cut up their food.*

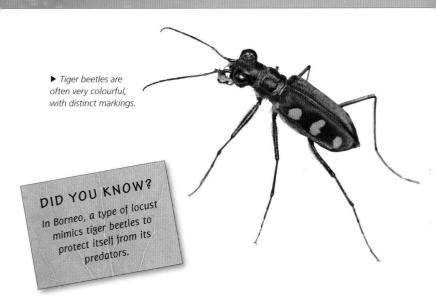

▶ Tiger beetles are often very colourful, with distinct markings.

DID YOU KNOW?
In Borneo, a type of locust mimics tiger beetles to protect itself from its predators.

These insects are predatory. Once they locate their prey, they pounce on it and use their jaws to tear it into pieces.

Tiger beetles taste awful and predators avoid eating them.

Females lay their eggs in burrows in the ground. The burrow can be almost 0.5 m deep.

The larvae have a pair of powerful and large jaws, which are used to capture small insects.

Some species of tiger beetles are endangered or nearing extinction. This is because of the lack of undisturbed sandy areas in which they can breed.

Stag beetle

🪰 **Stag beetles** are usually brown or black in colour but there are some species that are bright green and red.

🪰 **These beetles live** in damp wooded areas, especially near oak woodlands.

🪰 **Stag beetles** have mandibles (jaws), which resemble the antlers of a stag.

🪰 **Males** have long and ferocious-looking jaws. The jaws of females are not as long as those of the males.

▼ Stag beetles belong to the scarab beetle family, which contains over 20,000 species.

▶ *The female stag beetle lays her eggs in rotting wood. Larvae hatch and feed on wood for up to six years before they pupate.*

Males use their antlers to attract females. They rarely use their jaws to fight or defend themselves.

At dusk male stag beetles fly in search of females to mate with. They fly in an irregular fashion and are often misguided by bright lights.

The larvae of these insects feed on rotten wood and plant remains.

Larvae take a long time to develop into mature adults because the food on which they feed is not nutritious.

Adult stag beetles do not usually eat anything because they have enough reserve energy stored as fat. However, they sometimes feed on the sweet sap of trees.

DID YOU KNOW?

Stag beetles are also known as 'pinching bugs' because they can nip with their jaws and draw blood from human beings.

159

Rhinoceros beetle

🦌 **Rhinoceros beetles** are believed to be the strongest creatures on Earth. They can carry about 850 times their own weight.

🦌 **These beetles can grow** up to 13 cm in length.

🦌 **The preferred habitat** of rhinoceros beetles is tropical rainforests where the vegetation is thick and there is plenty of moisture in the atmosphere.

🦌 **Rhinoceros beetles** are named after the horns on their head, which resemble spikes.

🦌 **Only males** have horns. The larger the horn, the better are their chances of winning a mate's attention.

🦌 **The horns** are very strong and can pierce through the exoskeletons of insects.

🦌 **Rhinoceros beetles do not use** their horns for defending themselves from predators. Instead, they use them to fight with other males for food and to attract female beetles for mating.

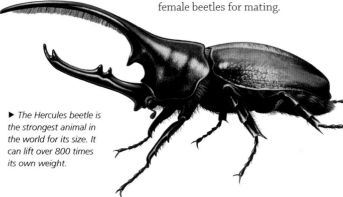

▶ The Hercules beetle is the strongest animal in the world for its size. It can lift over 800 times its own weight.

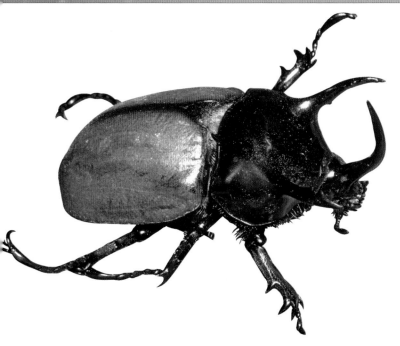

▲ *This rhinoceros beetle has three horns, but others have two or five horns. The very tough exoskeleton protects the beetle's body like a suit of armour.*

Rhinoceros beetles are nocturnal in nature and almost all their hunting and feeding activities take place at night.

These beetles help to keep the jungle clean and feed on plant sap and rotten fruits that have fallen to the ground.

Rhinoceros beetles are known to be fierce fighters. Natives in some parts of Thailand hold beetle fighting competitions to watch these beetles fight.

Ladybird beetle

> **Ladybird beetles**, or ladybugs, were dedicated to the Virgin Mary. They were known as 'beetle of Our Lady' during the medieval period.

> **Ladybirds are found** in temperate and tropical regions all over the world.

> **These beetles** are one of the most beneficial insects because they feed on insect pests that damage crops.

▼ *The number of spots on a ladybird differs from species to species. The two-spot ladybird is smaller than its seven-spotted cousin.*

Ladybirds are sometimes bred on a large scale and are then introduced into farms or greenhouses to get rid of pests. However, some species of ladybirds are herbivorous and are considered pests themselves.

These insects are easily mistaken for leaf beetles because of their similar colouring and spots.

▲ *Brightly coloured beetles, ladybirds have round bodies and hard wing cases, called elytra.*

When disturbed, ladybirds secrete a foul-smelling fluid, which causes a stain. This is called reflex-bleeding.

Both adults and larvae eat aphids, scale insects and other soft-bodied insects.

Ladybird larvae do not have wings. They are metallic blue in colour with bright yellow spots all over their body. Their bright colour warns birds not to eat them.

The halloween ladybird is a pumpkin-orange coloured beetle found in the USA during late October. It is named after Halloween since it is often seen during this festival.

Adult ladybirds hibernate in huge clusters in densely vegetated areas, usually at high altitudes.

True bugs

True bugs belong to the suborder Heteroptera of the order Hemiptera. There are at least 55,000 different kinds of bugs.

These bugs generally have two pairs of wings. The first pair is partially hard and protects the delicate membrane-like second pair of wings.

DID YOU KNOW?
Some people cultivate certain species of bugs to obtain dyes from them, while others relish bugs as food. Bugs are often harvested on a commercial scale for various purposes.

Some bugs do not have wings, while the nymphs of all true bugs are wingless.

True bugs have compound eyes and their mouthparts are adapted for sucking and piercing. Most bugs have beaks that are segmented into four or five parts.

Bugs undergo incomplete metamorphosis. There is no pupal stage and the bugs grow into adults by moulting again and again. The nymphs resemble the adult bugs.

Bugs can survive on land, in air, on the surface of water and even underwater. There are very few places where bugs do not live.

Some bugs can give out a very bad odour. This is a defence strategy.

Bugs feed on plant and animal juices. There are some bugs, such as bedbugs, which are parasites. They live by sucking blood from other animals.

Carnivorous bugs are predatory and help to control pests while herbivorous bugs are a threat to crops. Bugs can be cannibalistic and may feed on weaker individuals of their own kind.

▼ *The word 'bug' is sometimes used to mean any insect, but a true bug is an insect with piercing and sucking mouthparts, which are tucked beneath the head when not in use.*

Assassin bug

Assassin bugs are either black or brown or bright red and black in colour.

The wings of assassin bugs lie flat on their abdomen. These insects have long legs, which are adapted for running.

▼ Assassin bugs give out a pungent smell, which, along with their poisonous bite, protects them from their predators.

Assassin bugs are predatory. They grab their prey and 'assassinate' it by injecting venom. The venom paralyzes the prey and partially dissolves and disintegrates it. The bug then sucks the liquid food.

DID YOU KNOW?
The saliva of assassin bugs can cause temporary blindness in humans.

This venom is so powerful that caterpillars, which are much larger than assassin bugs, can be killed in seconds. An assassin bug may take several days to eat a large victim. Its front legs have powerful muscles for holding prey while sucking out their body fluid.

Assassin bugs have a powerful curved beak, which is used for sucking the blood of insects, larger animals and even humans.

Male and female assassin bugs are similar in appearance but sometimes the females do not have wings.

An assassin bug's bite is quite painful and can transmit germs and diseases. These bugs are known to spread a disease called Chagas' disease.

A species of assassin bug, known as the masked assassin bug, camouflages itself by sticking dirt to its body.

Squash bug

- **Squash bugs are so named** because they are a threat to squash and other related plants. They can usually be found in colours ranging from brown to black.

- **Some squash bugs** have leaflike extensions on their hind legs. This makes them look like dead leaves, which helps with camouflage. These bugs are called leaf-footed bugs.

- **With their powerful beaks**, squash bugs can easily pierce and suck fluids from plants and insects.

- **Squash bugs have scent glands** that emit a pungent smell. However, the odour is not as strong as that of stink bugs.

- **Although most** squash bugs are carnivorous, a few feed on both plants and insects, and some are strictly vegetarian.

- **While feeding**, the squash bug injects a toxic substance into the plant. As a result, the plant wilts and dies.

- **Squash bugs lay their eggs** in clusters on plants. The eggs are oval, flattish or elongated in shape.

- **The nymphs** that hatch from these eggs resemble black ants and moult four to five times before maturing into adults.

- **Farmers consider** squash bugs to be dangerous pests and adopt various measures to get rid of them.

DID YOU KNOW?
A rice field affected by squash bugs can be smelt from a considerable distance.

▼ The squash bug of North America feeds on the juices of cucumber, squash, melon, pumpkin and other gourds. It does not have leaflike back legs.

Cicada

- **Cicadas** belong to the order Homoptera and are related to true bugs. Most species of cicada are found in deserts, grasslands and forests.

- **Cicadas have** large and colourful wings. They hold their wings in a slanting position over their abdomen, like a tent.

- **Male cicadas emit** sounds similar to that of a knife grinder, a railway whistle and even to fat spitting in an overheated pan.

- **Male cicadas** sing loudly to attract females, with the help of special drumlike membranes called timbals. Female cicadas do not produce any sound because their timbals are not developed.

- **Large swarms of cicadas** attract birds, which feast on these insects.

- **Female cicadas** lay their eggs on plants and tree twigs. When the eggs hatch, the nymphs fall to the ground. They live underground for many years, feeding on the roots of plants. Later, they emerge from the ground, climb up trees and then moult.

- **Adult cicadas** do not live as long as the nymphs. They only survive a few weeks.

- **A species of cicada** known as the periodical cicada is found in America. It emerges from under the ground every 13 or 17 years. These insects are one of the longest-lived in the world.

▶ *Cicada eggs hatch into wingless nymphs. Most cicadas spend between one to three years as nymphs, growing and moulting as they gradually develop into adults.*

◄ Cicadas have four pairs of membranous wings, although the front pair of wings are twice the length of the back pair.

Spittlebug

▶ *Spittlebug nymphs produce 'cuckoo spit'
by giving off a sticky liquid and blowing it
into a frothy mass of white bubbles.*

Spittlebugs are different shades of yellow and brown. They have a triangular head, red eyes and spotted wings.

Also known as froghoppers, Spittlebugs have a froglike appearance. They are good jumpers but rarely fly, even though they have well-developed wings.

Adult spittlebugs have rather large heads in comparison to their small bodies.

Females lay their eggs in the stems of grasses and other plants.

These bugs are named after the spitlike frothy mass secreted by the nymphs. This froth is sometimes known as cuckoo-spit.

Spittlebug nymphs are not easy to spot because they are often hidden in cuckoo-spit on leaves.

Cuckoo-spit helps the nymphs to control their temperature and even prevents them from losing moisture and drying out.

DID YOU KNOW?
In Madagascar, spittlebugs discharge a clear liquid instead of foam, which falls to the ground like rain.

▶ Cuckoo-spit protects the spittlebug nymphs from predators.

Some spittlebug nymphs form delicate tubes about 10–12 mm in length. They attach these tubes along the sides of twigs and live there after filling them with spittle.

Spittlebugs are considered to be pests as they feed on the sap of plants.

▼ Adult spittlebugs do not produce foamy spittle like their nymphs. They spend their time hopping about like tiny frogs on the plants and shrubs from which they feed.

Mealybug

Mealybugs are very small insects up to 3 mm long. They are found in huge clusters on leaves, twigs and tree bark. These bugs are also called coccids.

Females do not usually have wings, eyes or legs and remain immobile on plants. They are always covered in a white sticky coating of their own secretion. This protective coating looks like cornmeal.

Males usually have one pair of delicate wings, well-developed legs and antennae, and no mouthparts.

▲ Female mealybugs secrete a mass of waxy threads as a protective covering. They are often wingless and legless, with reduced antennae.

▶ *Mealybug nymphs do not usually move after their first moult. They stay in one place, joined to plants only by their sucking mouthparts.*

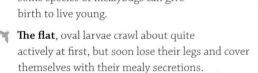

Female mealybugs never lay their eggs in the open. The eggs are attached to their bodies. However, some species of mealybugs can give birth to live young.

The flat, oval larvae crawl about quite actively at first, but soon lose their legs and cover themselves with their mealy secretions.

A male mealybug's hind wings are modified into tiny structures called halteres.

Mealybugs feed on the sap extracted from plant tissues and are considered to be pests of citrus trees and greenhouse plants.

These bugs can harm plants in many ways. Galls can form on plants, or their stems can become twisted and deformed.

Mealybugs produce a sugary substance known as honeydew. Ants often visit these insects for this sweet-tasting secretion.

Beetles, lacewings and caterpillars prey on mealybugs.

Aphid

🐦 **Aphids are related to cicadas**. They can be green, red or brown in colour and are also called greenfly.

🐦 **These bugs have** a large pear-shaped abdomen with two slender tubes called cornicles attached to it. The cornicles secrete wax.

🐦 **Aphids** may or may not have wings. Those with wings are weak fliers, but they can cover great distances with the help of air currents.

🐦 **Many aphids** live underground and suck sap from roots. Sometimes these insects depend upon ants to carry them through tunnels in the soil and leave them out on fresh roots.

▼ *Aphids produce a sugary substance that ants like to eat. In return, the ants protect the aphids from their predators, build shelters, 'graze' them in fresh pastures and even take them into their ant nests during bad weather.*

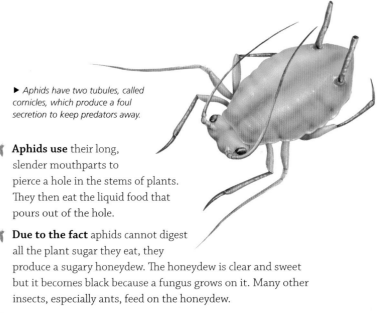

▶ Aphids have two tubules, called cornicles, which produce a foul secretion to keep predators away.

Aphids use their long, slender mouthparts to pierce a hole in the stems of plants. They then eat the liquid food that pours out of the hole.

Due to the fact aphids cannot digest all the plant sugar they eat, they produce a sugary honeydew. The honeydew is clear and sweet but it becomes black because a fungus grows on it. Many other insects, especially ants, feed on the honeydew.

Some aphids lay eggs but others can reproduce without mating. These aphids give birth to live young by the process of parthenogenesis.

Aphids breed in huge numbers. A single aphid can produce up to 100 young at a time.

Some aphids secrete long, curly strands of a waxlike substance from their cornicles. These aphids form dense colonies, which can be seen from many metres away.

Aphids can cause damage to plants. Their saliva causes plant leaves to fold, curl and even form galls.

Leafhopper

🦟 **Related to cicadas**, leafhoppers have a distinct leaflike shape and colour and are easy to recognize.

🦟 **Leafhoppers can survive** in almost any part of the world. They are terrestrial bugs and can be found in deserts as well as in marshy and moist places.

🦟 **Strong fliers**, leafhoppers are also capable of jumping considerable distances.

🦟 **If these insects** feed on plants, they can cause the leaves to curl and affect the plant's growth.

🦟 **Leafhoppers** are considered pests because they damage crops.

🦟 **Leafhoppers search for mates** by making special mating calls.

🦟 **Females lay their eggs** in slits made in plant stems. The eggs can remain dormant for a month. In some species, the eggs remain dormant for a year.

🦟 **Like aphids**, leafhoppers produce honeydew from the excess plant sap that they feed on.

🦟 **These bugs** communicate with each other by producing low frequency sounds, which humans cannot hear.

🦟 **Birds, reptiles and large insects**, such as wasps, are a threat to leafhoppers.

▲ Leafhoppers are
common jumping insects
that look like a narrow version
of an adult spittlebug. They are tiny
insects – only 2–15 mm long.

Stinkbug

- **Stinkbugs have glands** on their undersurface, from which they secrete a fluid. This fluid has a foul odour, which is why these insects are called stinkbugs.

- **Their scent** has a strong effect on many animals and protects them from predators.

- **Stinkbugs can be found** in many colours, such as green, grey, brown, red, black and yellow. They are one of the most notorious pests found in farmlands and orchards.

- **Some species** of stinkbugs produce a loud sound to defend themselves.

- **Stinkbugs have a compound** called glycerol in their blood. This prevents their blood from freezing in winter.

- **Many species** of stinkbug are active during the day, while others are nocturnal, especially the dark-coloured species, which live in thick grass or under leaves.

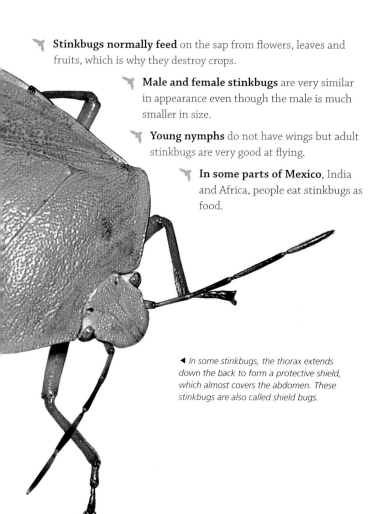

🐝 **Stinkbugs normally feed** on the sap from flowers, leaves and fruits, which is why they destroy crops.

🐝 **Male and female stinkbugs** are very similar in appearance even though the male is much smaller in size.

🐝 **Young nymphs** do not have wings but adult stinkbugs are very good at flying.

🐝 **In some parts of Mexico**, India and Africa, people eat stinkbugs as food.

◀ In some stinkbugs, the thorax extends down the back to form a protective shield, which almost covers the abdomen. These stinkbugs are also called shield bugs.

181

Lesser water boatman

▲ Lesser water boatmen are not buoyant enough to float, so when they stop swimming, they sink to the bottom. This is useful because they feed on the bottom of ponds, canals and ditches, using their shovel-like front legs to dig up food.

- **Lesser water boatmen** are aquatic insects and are usually found in ponds and other freshwater bodies, such as canals and ditches.

- **These bugs have powerful**, hairy legs and are named after their habit of using their legs as oars to 'row' themselves through the water.

DID YOU KNOW?

People in Mexico dry lesser water boatmen eggs and eat them. In some countries, lesser water boatmen are also sold as bird food.

- **Most species** of lesser water boatman can fly. However, these insects usually cling to water plants or live at the bottom of ponds.

- **Lesser water boatmen** do not have gills and have to come to the water's surface to breathe.

- **Hairs on the body** trap air bubbles. This helps lesser water boatmen to stay under water for long periods.

- **Lesser water boatmen feed** on algae, plants and decaying animal matter.

- **Some males** rub their legs together to make squeaky sounds that attract females.

- **The female** lays her eggs under water. The young nymphs that hatch from the eggs resemble the adults (without wings), but they moult five times before they become winged adults.

Backswimmer

🗲 **Backswimmers** spend almost their entire life floating in an upside down position in ponds.

🗲 **These insects use their legs like oars** and resemble rowing boats.

🗲 **While floating**, backswimmers identify direction with the help of light.

🗲 **Unlike other insects**, the underside of backswimmers is dark in colour while the top of the body is light. The dark colour helps to hide the backswimmer from predators.

🗲 **Backswimmers** come to the water's surface for air. They carry a bubble of air under their belly, which helps them to stay underwater for a long time. This air bubble gives them a silvery appearance.

🗲 **In appearance**, backswimmers look very similar to lesser water boatmen. However, lesser water boatmen float the right way up and feed mainly on plants. Backswimmers, in contrast, are predators.

DID YOU KNOW?

Also known as water bees, the backswimmer's bite is painful. Backswimmers have been known to bite humans.

🗲 **These insects** fly from one pond to another in search of food.

▲ Backswimmers spend almost all their time floating upside down.

Backswimmers feed on other water insects, worms and tadpoles.

When attacking, backswimmers inject toxins into their prey. This has a chemical reaction, which kills the prey.

Some species of backswimmers are known to hibernate. During winter, these insects are found moving under the surface of frozen water.

Water strider

Water striders are often found floating on still water and slow moving streams. They are one of the few insects that can survive in the sea and have even been found floating on the surface of the Pacific Ocean.

▼ *The long, thin legs of a water strider help to spread out its weight. The surface of the water bends into small dips around the end of each leg, but does not break.*

- **Water striders** seldom go underwater. Their long legs help them to skate and steer across the water. They are also called pond skaters.

- **These insects have six legs**, although it seems as if they have only four. The front two legs are short and are mainly used to grasp prey. The hind legs are very long and can be twice the length of the body.

- **Water striders have** long, slender, hairy legs, which end in a pad of water repellent hairs so they do not break through the surface of the water.

- **Some adults** have wings, while others are wingless.

- **Water striders feed** on insects that fall into the water and aquatic insects that come to the surface to breathe.

- **Water striders communicate** with each other by making vibrations and ripples on the water's surface.

- **Adults** hibernate throughout winter and mate in the spring.

DID YOU KNOW?
Water striders are also known as Jesus bugs because of their ability to walk on water. These insects move very quickly and can run across water. If they were as big as humans, they would move as fast as a jet plane.

Water scorpion

Water scorpions look very similar to land scorpions. They have forelegs that resemble pincers. The abdomen is also long like a scorpion's.

There are two types of water scorpion. One looks like a leaf, while the other is long and slender like a needle and is called a needle bug. Water scorpions are also called toebiters because they can sting people wading in the water.

Water scorpions live in plants at the water's edge. They move slowly and often stay still for many hours.

These insects are voracious eaters and feed on tadpoles, fish and other small aquatic animals. Even though they can swim for short distances, they usually keep still and lie in wait for their prey. When the prey comes near, they pounce on it.

The prey is injected with venom and paralyzed. Water scorpions are true bugs and can only suck fluids out of their prey.

Like most aquatic insects, water scorpions do not have gills and their body hair traps bubbles. These air bubbles help them to breathe underwater.

Water scorpions occasionally come to the surface to breathe. They have a breathing tube attached to the end of their body that is used as a snorkel. However, the larvae breathe through spiracles (breathing holes in the side of the body).

Male water scorpions rub their forelegs against their body to make chirping sounds in order to attract a female.

Females lay their eggs in slits made in plant stems. These eggs have tiny holes, which help them to breathe.

Water scorpions are active in summer, but they survive winter as well. They are found floating in ponds even when the temperature is very low.

▼ The water scorpion is a predator. Its legs are suited to catching prey, such as this tadpole, and its mouthparts are adapted to sucking fluids from the prey's body.

189

Termites, cockroaches, crickets and grasshoppers

Termite anatomy

Termites are believed to have evolved from an ancient cockroach-like ancestor at least 250 million years ago.

Termites live mainly in hot tropical countries such as Africa and Australia, but some do live in cooler places in America and Europe.

These insects are popularly known as white ants because termites and ants look similar, even though they are not related. However, they can be easily distinguished. Ants have elbowed antennae, while termites have straight antennae.

Termites also have two pairs of large wings, which overlap each other on their backs when at rest. These wings are equal in size, unlike those of ants. Termites belong to the insect order Isoptera, meaning 'equal wings'.

Leaving behind a stublike wing base, termites often shed their wings. Winged termites are called alates. They hatch once a year.

Termites are small and pale and avoid sunlight. Like all insects, they have a head, thorax and abdomen. The thorax has a broad joint with the abdomen, unlike the pointed 'waist' of ants, bees and butterflies.

▼ Initially, the queen lays a small number of eggs. As the colony matures, she can lay more eggs – as many as 36,000 eggs a day. The queen may grow to such a size that she can no longer move.

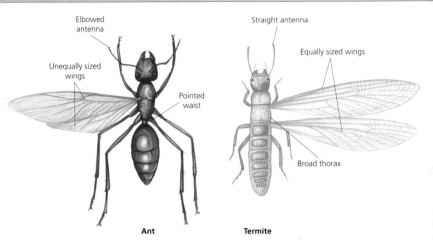

Elbowed antenna

Unequally sized wings

Pointed waist

Straight antenna

Equally sized wings

Broad thorax

Ant

Termite

▲ *A comparison of an ant and a termite. Although these insects are often mixed up, there are some key differences in their bodies.*

There are two main types of termites – ground termites (also called subterranean termites) and wood termites. Ground termites nest in soil and wood termites nest in wooden planks and other wooden structures.

The mouthparts of termites are modified for the purpose of chewing wood. They have antennae, which can be either beadlike or threadlike.

Termites have a very soft cuticle (an outer covering), which dries up easily. This is why they live in dark, warm and damp nests.

Some termites have protozoa (single-celled creatures) in their stomach. These help with the difficult process of digesting cellulose (a carbohydrate that contains glucose) present in plants and wood.

193

Social behaviour

🐦 **Termites** are social insects that live in well-organized groups or colonies. A termite colony is a highly integrated unit where each and every function is divided among the various termites.

🐦 **Small termite** colonies can have hundreds or thousands of termites, while a large colony can be home to millions of termites.

▼ *Termite mounds are incredibly complex constructions. They can reach 10 m tall and have air conditioning shafts built into them. These enable the termites to control the temperature of the nest to within one degree.*

Royal chamber where the queen termite lays eggs

Courtier workers look after the queen

Queen

Nursery termites care for eggs and larvae

Forager termites collect food

Cleaner termites repair the nest and get rid of wastes

There are different categories of termite in a colony – the king, the queen, workers and soldiers. All these categories are referred to as castes. The workers and soldiers cannot reproduce.

Workers form the major part of the colony's population. They work hard, taking care of the eggs and maintaining the nest, as well as foraging for food and feeding the young.

Soldiers defend the colony from predators. Two large jaws, which protrude from a hardened head, are used as weapons.

In a colony, termites communicate with each other about the direction and presence of food through vibrations, physical contact and chemical scents called pheromones.

Reproductives and soldiers produce a pheromone that helps them to maintain the caste balance of the colony. They lick the nymphs and transmit the pheromone that stops these nymphs from developing into reproductives and soldiers.

If the number of these termites goes down, they stop passing on the pheromone. This means that more reproductives and soldiers are produced, which restores the balance of the colony.

The king termite helps the queen to set up the colony and mates with her. The queen lays eggs and looks after the colony.

Workers and soldiers are the first nymphs to hatch from eggs so that they can build the nest and defend it. Once there are enough worker termites, the queen no longer looks after the young ones.

During early spring, winged reproductives can be seen flying and searching for an appropriate place to raise a new colony.

Termite facts

Termites feed on decaying wood, tree stumps, the roots of shrubs and other vegetation. They damage anything made of wood, including furniture, doors and windows.

If a termite colony becomes too big, swarming (moving in a large group) takes place. This is initiated by the winged adults of the colony, which are called 'alates'. Swarming can also take place because of climatic changes.

Some species may resort to cannibalism as a means of controlling their population.

Before swarming, the worker termites prepare tunnels and make holes inside the nest so that the alates can fly out.

When the alates leave the nest, the soldiers guard the entrance and defend them from predators. They also prevent the alates from re-entering.

Alates are weak fliers and are usually carried by the wind to different nesting grounds. This flight is called the nuptial flight.

Once the alates settle down in a nesting place, they shed their wings. The females produce a chemical to attract the males. The males and females then dig a hole and seal it. Mating takes place inside the hole.

▶ *Giant anteaters open termite mounds using their clawed forelimbs. They catch the termites using their long, sticky tongues, which can reach 60 cm in length.*

In tropical regions, the queen termites can lay eggs throughout the year. However, in temperate regions, the queens do not lay eggs in winter.

Soldier termites are blind. They defend themselves with their jaws, which function like scissors and can slice their enemies into pieces.

Termites can locate predators, such as anteaters, with their senses of touch and smell.

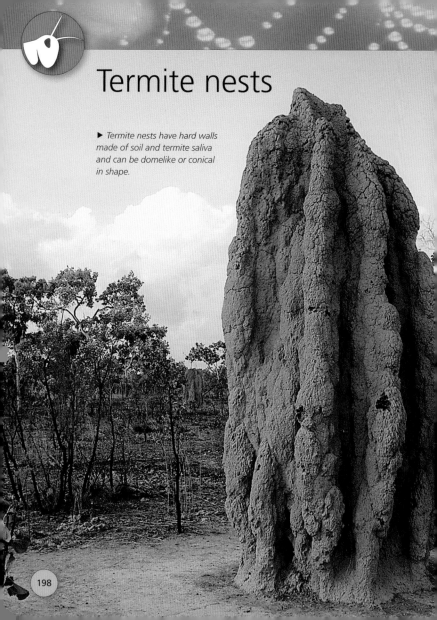

Termite nests

▶ Termite nests have hard walls made of soil and termite saliva and can be domelike or conical in shape.

Termites can nest anywhere they find humid and favourable conditions. They can nest underground or in hollow tree stumps, shrub roots, cellar walls, window frames, wooden posts and even in books.

These nests provide protection from extreme weather conditions and enemies. A large termite nest is called a termitarium.

Termites collect dirt, clay particles and chewed wood, which they glue together with saliva or excreta. They use this to build their nests.

Worker termites build the nests, which are damp, dark and sealed from the outside environment.

The nest is ventilated by pores in the nest walls and sometimes tall chimneys through which warm air from inside the nest can escape.

Termite nests have many chambers, called pockets, and a network of galleries that connects the horizontal layers of chambers.

Nests can be completely underground. However, some nests rise above the ground and are known as termite hills or mounds. These hills are a regular sight in tropical regions. Certain African termites can build mounds that are 8–9 m high.

Termites build very striking nests that may be very large or have a complex architecture. They can also build cryptic nests that are difficult to find.

Ground termite

Social insects, ground termites live in large groups or colonies. They are also known as subterranean termites because they nest in soil.

Ground termites live underground. A colony can contain over one million termites, although it may be smaller in size. The maximum capacity of a colony is reached in four to five years.

In a ground termite colony, there are reproductives (king and queen), soldiers and workers.

Once the colony reaches its full capacity, the new reproductives fly away to start their own colonies. They pair up and mate to start a new colony.

Soldiers have elongated sharp jaws, which are used for defence against enemies, such as ants. They can tear, slice and kill their enemies with their powerful jaws.

Workers feed the soldiers as they cannot feed themselves. They also take care of the nest and the young ones.

Ground termites dig mud tunnels, called mud tubes, through which they travel underground to look for food. They leave behind a scent trail for other members, which contains information about the location of the food. Soldiers and workers bang their heads against tunnel walls to tell other termites about food sources and enemy attacks.

These termites have a thin outer covering called an exoskeleton. If this dries up, they die. Therefore, they always maintain contact with the moist soil around their nests.

Ground termites feed on wood and products made from wood, including books and paper. They are a serious threat to buildings and other wooden structures. People use techniques such as termite scanning and chemical treatment to keep termites away from wooden structures.

▼ *Worker termites are normally small, soft and pale. Soldier termites defend the colony and are equipped with large heads and strong jaws.*

Wood termite

Wood termites are known to be very destructive as they destroy large wooden structures from the inside. They can be a threat to houses and furniture.

These insects are also called primitive termites. There are various types of wood termite – dry-wood, damp-wood and rotten-wood termites. They are differentiated by their nesting habits.

DID YOU KNOW?
Wood termites do not need external moisture or contact with the soil for survival. They can survive on the little moisture they get from the wood on which they nest.

Dry-wood termites can withstand the excessively dry condition of wood. They infest the dry, seasoned wood in houses and other places.

These termites eject pellets that look like wood dust from their excavations in the timber in buildings. So they are also called powder-post termites.

Damp-wood termites need constant high moisture such as is found in dead or decaying logs and the branches of live trees.

Wood termites build small colonies ranging from a few hundred to 1000 termites. Damp-wood termites usually nest in the wood and as soon as the wood is consumed, the entire colony dies.

Rotten-wood termites produce sandlike particles that are found beside wooden structures and are a clue to their presence.

Wood termites have a unique caste system. Instead of true workers, they have false workers, which are old nymphs of the colony. They take care of the nests temporarily.

People use a chemical called termiticide to coat and protect wood from termite attacks. Fumigation is also used as a preventive measure to keep these pests away.

▼ *Wood is difficult to digest. Wood termites have bacteria and other single-celled organisms in their guts to help them digest tough plant material and wood.*

203

Cockroaches

🦟 **Cockroaches belong** to the order Blattodea of class Insecta. There are about 4000 known species of cockroaches. Some well known cockroaches are oriental black beetles and croton bugs.

🦟 **Cockroaches** are found everywhere, especially in bat caves, peoples' homes, under stones, in thick grass and on trees and plants. The cockroaches found in caves are usually blind.

▲ *Female cockroaches lay their eggs in purselike capsules. Each egg case contains about 15 eggs.*

🦟 **These insects** may be winged or wingless. Adult cockroaches can be 1–9 cm long. They are nocturnal and prefer dark and damp places.

🦟 **Cockroaches are swift creatures** and can run extremely fast. Their legs are adapted for quick movement. They have flat, oval bodies that help them to hide in narrow cracks in walls and floors.

DID YOU KNOW?

The name cockroach comes from the Spanish word cucaracha. These insects adapt quickly to changes in the environment and can even survive a nuclear explosion.

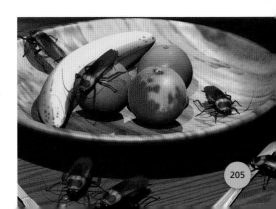

Most cockroach species are omnivorous. Their main food is plant sap, dead animals and vegetable matter but they will even eat shoe polish, glue, soap and ink.

Adults can live for up to two years. Males and females are very similar in appearance but males have a pair of bristle-like styli.

In some species, females release pheromones or produce a hissing sound and wave their abdomen to attract male cockroaches.

Females can lay up to 30–40 eggs at a time and can reproduce four times in a year. They store the eggs in a brownish egg case called an ootheca. The cockroach can either carry this egg case along with her or hide it somewhere. Young cockroaches are called nymphs.

Cockroaches play an important role in balancing the environment by digesting a wide range of waste substances. They decompose forest and animal waste matter. However, household cockroaches can contaminate food and spread diseases among humans.

▶ Cockroaches are not dirty creatures. They work hard to keep themselves clean in order to preserve a coating of wax and oils that prevents them from drying out. It is the bacteria they carry that makes them dangerous.

Madagascan hissing cockroach

Madagascan hissing cockroaches are found on the island of Madagascar, off the south-east coast of Africa. They are large, wingless insects, famous for the loud hissing sound that they make. These hisses are loud enough for people to hear.

These cockroaches are chocolate brown in colour, with dark orange marks on their abdomen. Adults can grow up to 10 cm in length.

▼ Hissing cockroaches make their distinctive noise by pushing air out of a pair of breathing holes in the side of their body. They have spiky legs for grip and protection.

A male cockroach can distinguish between familiar males and strangers from the hissing sound that they make.

Males look different from the females. They have a large, hornlike structure behind their heads and are more aggressive than the females. They also have hairy antennae, unlike the smooth antennae of the females.

DID YOU KNOW?

Male hissing cockroaches are territorial. They fight amongst themselves by ramming and pushing with their horns and abdomens. Once the fight is over, the winner makes loud hissing sounds to declare victory.

These cockroaches feed on dead animal matter, waste food or ripe fruits.

Females can produce 30–60 eggs, which they store in an egg sac, either inside or outside their body. The eggs hatch into nymphs.

The nymphs of hissing cockroaches moult six times in a period of seven months before maturing into adults. While moulting, the skin of a cockroach splits down the middle of its back and the cockroach slowly wriggles out.

Newly moulted cockroaches are whitish but their colour darkens within a few hours. Hissing cockroaches live for two to five years.

Madagascan hissing cockroaches can be easily bred in homes and classrooms. For this reason, they are ideal for classroom study.

Oriental cockroach

- **Oriental cockroaches** are seasonal insects and can be most easily spotted during the spring and summer. They are found in damp basements, drains, leaky pipes and kitchen sinks.

- **These cockroaches** are dark brown or black in colour and so they are sometimes called 'black beetles'. Adults can grow up to 3.5 cm in length.

- **This cockroach** is sometimes called the 'shad roach' because its young appear in large numbers when shad (a type of fish) are swimming into fresh waters to breed.

- **Males** have short wings but females are wingless.

- **Females** do have small wing stubs. This is what makes them different from their own nymphs.

- **A female** can produce five to ten egg cases (oothecae) in her lifetime. Each egg case contains about ten eggs.

- **Young cockroach nymphs** hatch from the egg cases in six to eight weeks and mature in 6–12 months. Adult cockroaches can live for up to one year.

- **Oriental cockroaches** have cerci at the end of the abdomen. These are important sensory organs.

DID YOU KNOW?

Oriental cockroaches can survive for up to one month without food, as long as water is available. Adults have a lifespan of about one year.

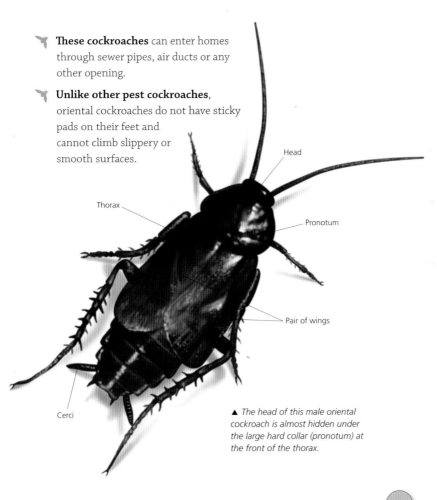

- **These cockroaches** can enter homes through sewer pipes, air ducts or any other opening.

- **Unlike other pest cockroaches**, oriental cockroaches do not have sticky pads on their feet and cannot climb slippery or smooth surfaces.

Head

Thorax

Pronotum

Pair of wings

Cerci

▲ The head of this male oriental cockroach is almost hidden under the large hard collar (pronotum) at the front of the thorax.

209

Death's head cockroach

▲ *Adult death's head cockroaches have yellow-and-black markings.*

- **Large insects**, death's head cockroaches measure 5–8 cm in length. These cockroaches are mostly found in the Americas.

- **Death's head cockroaches** are named after the strange markings on their thorax. These markings look like skulls or vampires.

DID YOU KNOW?
Death's head cockroaches make good pets and are popular among cockroach lovers.

- **These insects** are also known as the palmetto bug or giant death's head cockroach.

- **Death's head cockroaches live mostly** in tropical forests or bat caves but sometimes they are also found in buildings.

- **These cockroaches** are brownish in colour with yellow and black marks on their body. While adults are beautifully coloured, the nymphs are dark in colour, although newly moulted nymphs are whitish.

- **The wings** are very long and cover their abdomen. The nymphs are wingless.

- **Females carry the eggs** inside their bodies and give birth to live young that hatch from the eggs.

- **Cockroaches are scavengers** and are active at night. Decaying plant and animal matter are their favourite food.

Crickets

Crickets belong to the order Orthoptera and closely resemble grasshoppers. These insects are found almost everywhere – in fields, forests and gardens.

Crickets have flattened bodies and long antennae and measure up to 5 cm. Although all crickets have wings, some species do not fly. They can only hop from one place to another.

These insects make chirping sounds that attract females and warn rival males to keep away.

Crickets produce these sounds by rubbing the bases of their specially modified forewings.

▼ Crickets hatch out into nymphs that look like miniature adults without wings. They go through up to ten or more moults as they develop into winged adults.

Crickets are nocturnal and have keen hearing and eyesight. Compound eyes help crickets see far and in many directions at the same time. Round, flat hearing organs are found on the front legs.

Crickets are omnivorous and feed on crops, vegetables, flowers, green plants, small animals, clothes and each other.

Females have long needle-like ovipositors to lay eggs. They carry the eggs until they find a safe place where the eggs can hatch into nymphs.

Some species of crickets are considered pests because they eat crops and deposit their eggs on them.

In some parts of the world, crickets are thought to be a sign of good luck. For this reason, some people keep crickets as pets.

▲ Crickets are common insects that are found nearly everywhere.

Cave cricket

Cave crickets are named after their habit of living in caves and other dark and damp places.

Cave crickets are also known as camel crickets because they have a hump on their back.

Very long hind legs give cave crickets a spider-like appearance. Their strong hind legs make them good jumpers.

Cave crickets are brown in colour and have long antennae. They do not have wings.

These insects cannot chirp or make sounds because they are wingless. Crickets normally produce a high-pitched sound by rubbing their wings together.

Cave crickets are omnivorous and feed on decaying organic matter, plants and vegetables.

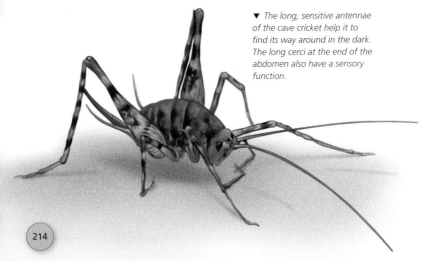

▼ The long, sensitive antennae of the cave cricket help it to find its way around in the dark. The long cerci at the end of the abdomen also have a sensory function.

▲ As well as caves, cave crickets are also found in wells, rotten logs, hollow trees and under damp leaves and stones.

In the spring, females lay their eggs in soil. The nymphs and adults spend the winter in sheltered areas.

Cave crickets are sometimes troublesome in buildings and homes, especially in basements.

These insects can damage articles stored in boxes, garages and laundry rooms.

215

Grasshoppers

Grasshoppers are green or brown in colour. Some species change colours in different seasons. The body is divided into head, thorax and abdomen. Grasshoppers have six legs, a pair of wings and compound eyes.

Found almost everywhere except in the polar regions, grasshoppers prefer to live in green fields, meadows and forest areas.

There are three types of grasshoppers – long-horned, short-horned and pygmy. Bush crickets are also known as long-horned grasshoppers.

Grasshoppers make a loud noise during the mating season to attract a mate or scare away rivals.

▶ When a grasshopper jumps, it uses its powerful leg muscles to propel its body forwards.

DID YOU KNOW?

When captured, grasshoppers spit a brown liquid to protect themselves from their predators. In some parts of the world, this brown liquid is known as tobacco juice.

After mating, the female lays her eggs in low bushes or digs a hole in the soil with her abdomen to deposit eggs from her ovipositor. She covers her eggs with a hard shell covering called an eggpod.

Grasshoppers are herbivorous. They feed on a variety of plants, grasses and crops. They use their mandibles to chew food.

These insects pose a serious threat to crops. A large group of grasshoppers can destroy an entire crop.

Flies, spiders, toads and reptiles prey on grasshoppers and even eat their eggs.

In some parts of the world, grasshoppers are considered a delicacy. They are ground into a meal, and sometimes fried or roasted and dipped in honey.

Locust

Locusts are found all over the world except in cold regions. Dark brown in colour, their average length is less than 2.5 cm.

Locusts live in fields, open woods or arid areas. They can fly for up to 20 hours, using reserves of fat stored in their bodies.

These insects are migratory in nature and travel great distances. They can be highly destructive of crops. A large swarm can consume 3000 tonnes of green plants in a single day.

Locusts breed very quickly compared to other insects. Some well known species are the desert locust, the red-legged locust and the Carolina locust.

Females lay their eggs in the soil. The nymphs are wingless and small in size. A female locust can lay 20 eggs at a time.

A locust eats an amount of food equivalent to its own weight every day. It feeds on crops, weeds, grass or other plants.

◀ *A locust can use its powerful leg muscles to jump ten times its own body length.*

▲ *This photograph, taken in Morocco, in 1954, shows people using poison bait in an attempt to combat locust swarms.*

DID YOU KNOW?

A locust swarm may occupy 26–777 sq km. Such swarms cast a shadow on the ground and appear like a huge black cloud.

Locusts have two phases – solitary and gregarious. In the solitary phase, locusts do not breed in large numbers and confine themselves to their surroundings. In the gregarious phase, the insects reproduce and grow quickly in the presence of an abundant food supply.

In the gregarious phase, the locusts accumulate in large numbers. As a result, the habitat where they stay is not sufficient to support and sustain them. Therefore, these insects migrate in search of new feeding grounds. This phenomenon is called swarming.

In some tribal groups, dried locusts are eaten as food.

219

Stick insect

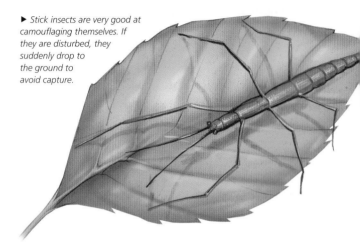

▶ Stick insects are very good at camouflaging themselves. If they are disturbed, they suddenly drop to the ground to avoid capture.

Stick insects belong to the order Phasmatodea. They look like leafless sticks and branches and are also called walking sticks.

These insects are green or brown in colour and spend their time clinging to trees, plants and shrubs.

Stick insects are excellent at camouflaging themselves, especially when they keep perfectly still or sway with the wind.

Some tropical species of stick insect have sharp spines on their legs, which blend in with the thorns of plants. If threatened, they can stab their enemies. They also change their colour like chameleons, depending on the humidity and temperature.

🦟 **Stick insects are active at night**, when they feed on foliage.

🦟 **Females are larger** than the males. Males can fly but the females can only glide.

🦟 **Females produce pheromones** to attract males. A single female can lay about 1000 eggs in its lifetime. They scatter their eggs randomly or hide them in order to protect them.

🦟 **Asiatic stick insects** are the longest stick insects, measuring more than 30 cm.

🦟 **Stick insects** can regenerate lost legs. If old limbs are cut off they can grow new ones.

▶ *Including its antennae and legs, the giant stick insect can measure over 50 cm in length.*

DID YOU KNOW?

Stick insects lie motionless and pretend to be dead to save themselves from their predators. This is called catalepsis.

223

Leaf insect

Leaf insects belong to the order Phasmatodea and are most common in Southeast Asia.

These insects have a unique appearance. Their bodies are flat, irregular in shape and resemble a leaf. These insects are about 10 cm in length and sometimes have brown or yellow patches on their body.

Females are much larger than males. They do not have hind wings and cannot fly but they do have leaflike forewings.

The female can lay eggs without mating with the male. This is called parthenogenesis.

A female scatters her eggs on the ground. These eggs have a hard outer shell and resemble seeds, so predators do not feed on them.

The eggs hatch in the spring.

Leaf insects are herbivorous and feed only on green leaves and other parts of plants.

Rodents, birds and other insects feed on leaf insects.

Leaf insects are good at camouflage and hiding from predators. They move very slowly and mimic the foliage on which they live.

▶ *This leaf insect would be very hard for predators to spot among green leaves, as long as it remained completely still.*

Damselfly

▲ *The large compound eyes of a damselfly bulge out to the side. Damselflies also have long legs, which they use to hold insects captured in flight. Their legs are not suited to walking.*

- **Damselflies** belong to the order Odonata and suborder Zygoptera. They have long, slender bodies and four long wings. They are weak fliers and timid predators.

- **These insects are beautiful**, slender cousins of dragonflies but are not as ferocious. They have compound eyes and excellent eyesight.

DID YOU KNOW?

Damselflies capture their prey with the help of their legs, folding them like a basket to form a trap. Once the insect is trapped it is transferred to the damselfly's mouth.

- **Damselflies** are usually found near water and their nymphs live in the water until they mature into adults.

- **Mosquitoes**, midges, gnats and small water insects are the preferred food of damselflies.

- **Damselfly nymphs** have external gills on the tip of their abdomen for breathing underwater. In dragonfly nymphs, these gills are internal.

- **Males and females** mate during flight or over shallow water. While mating, a male carries a female around to allow her to collect sperm from the front of his abdomen. After mating, females deposit their eggs in and around water.

- **The lifespan** of a damselfly is around one year but it can live up to two years.

- **During winter**, damselflies hibernate to survive the cold weather.

227

Dragonfly

- **Dragonflies are named** after their fierce jaws, which they use for catching prey.

- **These insects can grow up** to 12 cm in length. They have multi-coloured, long, slender bodies with two pairs of veined wings.

- **Larger dragonflies** are called hawkers, while the smaller ones are called darters.

- **Adult dragonflies** survive on land but their nymphs live underwater. They cannot survive harsh winters.

▶ Dragonflies have huge compound eyes, which cover their entire head.

DID YOU KNOW?

Dragonflies are one of the fastest insects. They can fly up to 50 km/h. The design and mechanism of a helicopter was probably inspired by a dragonfly.

The lifespan of a dragonfly ranges from six months to more than seven years.

Males and females mate while they fly. Once they have mated, the female dragonfly deposits her eggs in water or inside water plants.

A female dragonfly lays up to 100,000 eggs at a time. The eggs hatch into nymphs, which feed on fish, tadpoles and other small aquatic animals.

Dragonflies are beneficial to humans. They prey on mosquitoes, flies and many small insects that are pests.

Experts have found dragonfly fossils that are more than 300 million years old. These prehistoric dragonflies were as big as crows.

Lacewing

🦟 **Lacewings** are delicate green or brown insects that are named after their thin, translucent, lacelike wings.

🦟 **These insects have long**, threadlike antennae and their eyes are bright golden yellow or brown in colour.

🦟 **Birds and other predators** avoid lacewings because they give off a pungent odour similar to garlic.

🦟 **Lacewings are not good fliers** because their wings are too weak to support their weight for long distances. These insects are often seen fluttering about clumsily.

🦟 **A lacewing lays** a large number of eggs at a time. The eggs are white in colour and are glued to a twig or leaf. Green lacewings secrete a thin white stalk for each egg.

🦟 **Lacewing larvae** feed on small insects. They eat a lot of aphids and are also known as aphid lions. These insects are sometimes used to control the population of aphids in crop fields.

🦟 **The larvae of lacewings** are sometimes reared commercially to get rid of pests. Apart from aphids, these larvae feed on mealybugs, leafhoppers, caterpillars, moths and other insects. The larvae can become cannibalistic if there is not enough food.

🦟 **Lacewing larvae** have 'jaws', which make them resemble alligators. These jaws are used to suck the body fluids of the prey after injecting it with paralyzing venom.

▲ A lacewing has two similar pairs of wings, which are covered with a delicate network of veins. When the lacewing rests, it holds its wings together like a roof over its body.

Some lacewing larvae camouflage themselves with debris, including the skin and other remains of their prey.

Many species of adult lacewings do not eat other insects. Instead, they feed on nectar, pollen and honeydew.

Praying mantis

Closely related to cockroaches, praying mantises belong to the order Mantodea.

Praying mantises get their name from their posture. This insect holds its front legs together as if it were praying.

▼ *A praying mantis moves its long front legs very rapidly to grab its prey. Sharp spines stop the prey from escaping.*

DID YOU KNOW?
A female praying mantis often eats the male while mating!

🪰 **These insects** can grow up to 6.5 cm in length. They have triangular heads that can turn in a full circle. They are generally green or brown in colour.

🪰 **Praying mantises have good** camouflage to protect themselves from predators. Their body colour blends with their environment. A species called the Asiatic rose mantis even looks like flower petals. For this reason, it is also called the orchid mantis.

🪰 **Females are larger** than the males. They lay their eggs inside an egg case (ootheca) during the autumn.

🪰 **Females secrete** a sticky substance to stick their eggs to plant stems and tree twigs. Nymphs hatch from these eggs in the spring or summer.

🪰 **Praying mantises** are carnivorous and feed on insects, such as butterflies, moths and grasshoppers. They can even attack small lizards, frogs and birds. Small mantises can become cannibalistic, especially when there is no food.

🪰 **These insects** have a habit of silently watching and stalking prey before attacking. While feeding, a praying mantis holds its prey with its front legs.

🪰 **Praying mantises are useful** to humans. They protect crops by feeding on pests. Sometimes farmers buy them for pest control. These insects are often kept as pets, even though large praying mantises have a painful bite.

Mantisfly

Mantisflies are named after their folded pair of front legs, which look like those of praying mantises. Although these insects look similar, they are not related.

These insects are not common and are found in tropical regions.

Mantisflies, along with lacewings and antlions, belong to the order Neuroptera.

Mantisflies lay their rose-coloured eggs on slender plant stalks.

The mantisfly has a complicated development cycle. It has two growth stages as a larva and two more stages as a pupa.

One species of mantisfly has larvae that are a parasite of wolf spiders.

A single larva enters the spider's sac and preys upon the egg or young.

The larva pierces the egg or spider with its pointed mouthparts and feeds on its body fluids. The larva then pupates inside the spider's egg sac.

Unaware of the presence of the parasite mantisfly, the parent spider watches over the cocoon.

Some mantisflies mimic wasps and bees for protection.

Mantisflies are predatory like praying mantises and have similar feeding habits.

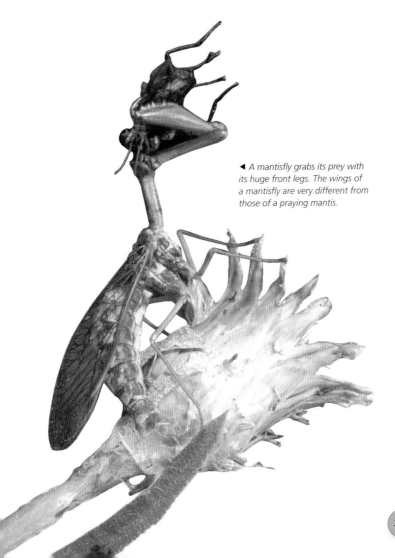

◄ A mantisfly grabs its prey with its huge front legs. The wings of a mantisfly are very different from those of a praying mantis.

Antlion

Antlions are named after the larva's habit of feeding on ants and other insects. Adult antlions feed on pollen or nectar or do not feed at all.

Antlions resemble dragonflies. They both have long slender bodies and four delicate wings. However, unlike dragonflies, antlions are nocturnal insects.

These insects are found in damp areas where vegetation is thick. Antlions are also found near riverbeds.

Some antlion larvae make a pit in the sand by moving around in a spiral path and throwing out sand.

While making the pit, the larva leaves behind squiggly doodles on the sand. For this reason, antlions are also known as doodlebugs.

▼ An antlion larva waits at the bottom of its pit trap for an unsuspecting ant to fall down into its pincer-like jaws.

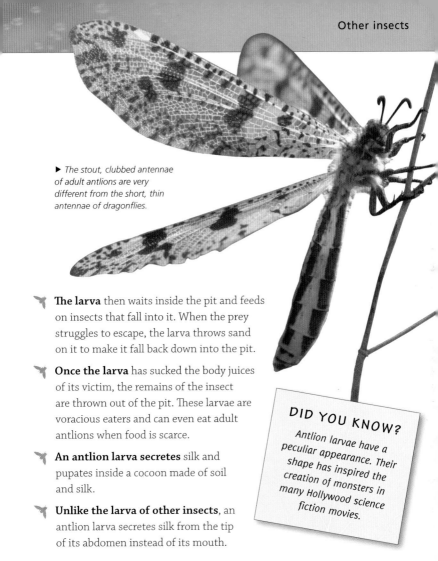

▶ The stout, clubbed antennae of adult antlions are very different from the short, thin antennae of dragonflies.

- **The larva** then waits inside the pit and feeds on insects that fall into it. When the prey struggles to escape, the larva throws sand on it to make it fall back down into the pit.

- **Once the larva** has sucked the body juices of its victim, the remains of the insect are thrown out of the pit. These larvae are voracious eaters and can even eat adult antlions when food is scarce.

- **An antlion larva secretes** silk and pupates inside a cocoon made of soil and silk.

- **Unlike the larva of other insects**, an antlion larva secretes silk from the tip of its abdomen instead of its mouth.

DID YOU KNOW?
Antlion larvae have a peculiar appearance. Their shape has inspired the creation of monsters in many Hollywood science fiction movies.

237

Stonefly

🐝 **Stoneflies are an ancient order** of insects that has been around for nearly 300 million years.

🐝 **Stonefly nymphs** cling to stones in clear mountain streams or lakes. They are eaten by fish and are also used as fish bait.

🐝 **Some stonefly nymphs** breathe through gills that are present near their legs. Others obtain oxygen through their body surface.

DID YOU KNOW?
Some male stoneflies attract females by drumming their abdomen against a hard surface. For this reason, these insects are popularly known as 'primitive drummers'.

🐝 **Adult stoneflies** are terrestrial, which means that they live on land. However, they never wander too far from water, spending their time crawling over stones. This is how their name originates.

🐝 **Female stoneflies** deposit their eggs in deep water. To prevent the eggs from floating away, they stick them to rocks with a sticky secretion.

▼ *A stonefly lives for up to two or three years.*

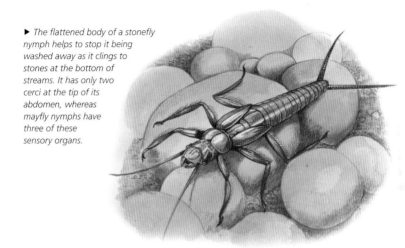

▶ The flattened body of a stonefly nymph helps to stop it being washed away as it clings to stones at the bottom of streams. It has only two cerci at the tip of its abdomen, whereas mayfly nymphs have three of these sensory organs.

A stonefly nymph resembles an adult but does not have wings and its reproductive organs are not as well-developed. These nymphs grow into adult stoneflies and crawl out of the water.

Stonefly nymphs feed on underwater plants, such as algae and lichens. Some species are carnivorous and feed on aquatic insects. Adults may not feed at all, although some eat algae and pollen.

Fish often attack female stoneflies when they try to deposit their eggs in streams.

Stoneflies are sensitive to water pollution. Experts use these insects to study the level of water purity.

Scorpionfly

Scorpionflies are a small group of insects with dark spots on their two pairs of membranous wings. These primitive insects have been around for 250 million years.

The rear body part of some males is curled upwards, similar to a scorpion's. Only males resemble scorpions.

Adult scorpionflies have modified mouthparts. They have a long beak pointing downwards.

Scorpionflies feed on live as well as dead insects. Some also feed on pollen, nectar and plants.

▼ Male scorpionflies have a large sting on a long curved tail. It looks like the sting of a scorpion but is harmless.

▶ A distinctive
feature of scorpionflies
is their elongated head with a
long 'beak', which ends in biting jaws.

Predators, scorpionflies often steal their food from spiders' webs. They catch their prey with their hind legs.

While mating, a male scorpionfly secretes a sweet, sticky secretion, on which the female scorpionfly feeds.

The female lays her eggs in wooden crevices and soil. The eggs hatch and the larvae live and pupate in loose soil or waste matter.

Scorpionfly larvae feed on dead and rotten plant and animal matter. Some larvae also feed on small insects.

Scorpionflies are often considered helpful to humans because they keep the environment clean by feeding on dead insects.

241

Mayfly

▲ *Adult mayflies have pale yellow bodies with brown stripes.*

Mayflies belong to the order Ephemeroptera – *ephemeros* means 'one day' and *pteron* means 'wing'. They are slender insects and measure up to 4 cm in length.

Easily spotted around streams and ponds, mayflies are characterized by triangular, membranous forewings and smaller, round hind wings.

Mayflies have soft, fragile bodies and also have two or three long, threadlike tails.

- **Even after** their wings become functional, mayflies moult. This is the pre-adult stage.

- **While resting**, mayflies hold their wings vertically and not in a rooflike position as other insects do.

- **Male mayflies** 'dance' in large swarms to attract females.

- **A female mayfly** lays her eggs in water by dipping her abdomen into the water while in flight.

- **Strongly attracted** to light, mayflies gather around lights on roads and streets.

- **Adult mayflies** do not bite humans but their huge swarms are a nuisance.

▼ Mayfly nymphs are good swimmers and live for two to three years underwater. They mostly feed on plant matter that has settled at the bottom of the river.

Flea

- **Fleas belong** to the order Siphonaptera. They are ectoparasites – parasites that live on the outside of their host.

- **Small wingless insects**, fleas measure 0.1–1 cm in length. These insects feed only on the blood of birds and mammals, including humans.

- **Bloodsucking pests**, fleas carry various deadly diseases. They transmit bubonic plague, which killed half the population of Europe in the mid 1300s.

- **When rats** die of bubonic plague, fleas infected with the plague bacilli seek food elsewhere. These fleas may transmit the disease to humans.

- **Fleas do not infest** monkeys, horses or apes.

- **Infestation by fleas** causes severe inflammation of the skin and itching. Animals heavily infested by fleas may die of a flea bite or severe blood loss.

- **Fleas** are themselves subject to parasitism by external mites and internal nematode worms.

DID YOU KNOW?

Flea larvae may remain in their cocoons for months until they sense the movement of an animal nearby.

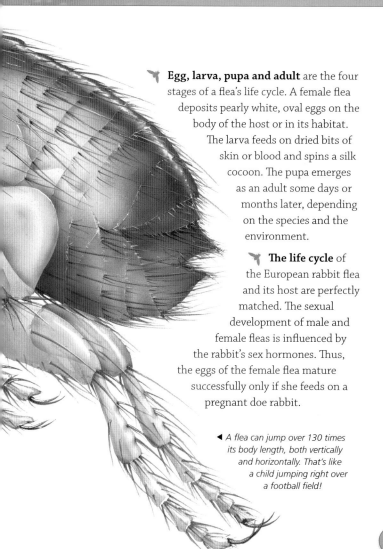

Egg, larva, pupa and adult are the four stages of a flea's life cycle. A female flea deposits pearly white, oval eggs on the body of the host or in its habitat. The larva feeds on dried bits of skin or blood and spins a silk cocoon. The pupa emerges as an adult some days or months later, depending on the species and the environment.

The life cycle of the European rabbit flea and its host are perfectly matched. The sexual development of male and female fleas is influenced by the rabbit's sex hormones. Thus, the eggs of the female flea mature successfully only if she feeds on a pregnant doe rabbit.

◀ A flea can jump over 130 times its body length, both vertically and horizontally. That's like a child jumping right over a football field!

245

Lice

🪰 **Many parasites** are capable of living off humans. They can infest hair, body or blood. Lice are just one type of parasite that thrives on the human body.

🪰 **Human lice belong** to the order Anoplura and a group known as sucking lice.

🪰 **Lice are small wingless insects** measuring up to 11 mm long. Two types of lice that frequently affect humans are the head louse and the body louse.

🪰 **The head louse** commonly infests school children but is also found on adults. The easiest way to get rid of them is to comb the hair thoroughly with a very fine 'nit' comb and use a treatment such as tea tree oil. Lice are more common on clean hair.

🪰 **A louse's body** is flattened, which helps it to lie close to the skin. The head louse attaches itself to the hair or scalp with the help of claws on its legs.

🪰 **Lice feed** on human blood. They have three needle-like structures or stylets, which can pierce the skin. These are held back by a specially adapted tongue.

🪰 **After piercing** the skin, the lice suck the blood with a pumping action of their throat. When the stylets are not in use, they are retracted into a pocket just behind the louse's mouth.

🪰 **Lice frequently feed on blood** and each feeding takes a few minutes.

An adult head louse may also be found in any facial hair, but they are almost never found below the neck. Head lice are transmitted by direct contact with an infested person or by using infested articles, such as headgear, combs, brushes or scarves.

A single female louse can lay five to ten eggs per day. Dead lice have even been discovered on the hair of ancient Egyptian mummies.

▼ The eggs or 'nits' of a head louse are firmly attached to the base of hairs, especially behind the ears and on the back of the neck.

247

Book louse

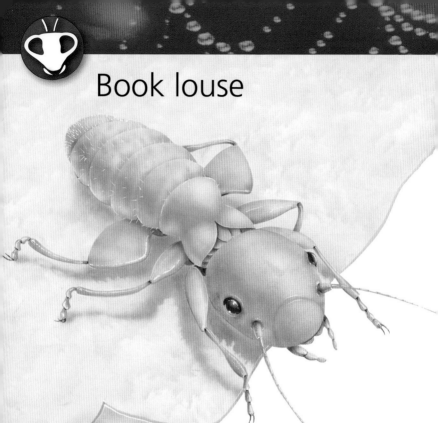

▲ *Book lice are so small that they are almost invisible to the naked eye. They can, however, destroy valuable collections of books by eating the glue that binds the pages.*

Book lice are small, colourless insects measuring 1–4 mm. They look like lice but are not true lice.

- **Soft-bodied**, transparent and usually wingless, they infest books, paper and cardboard boxes, especially those that are stored in dark and damp places. Book lice belong to the order Psocoptera.

- **The head and abdomen** appear large, while the thorax is narrow. Book lice have long, threadlike antennae and chewing mouthparts. Their eyes are large and protrude from the sides of the head.

- **Book lice** do not bite humans or animals. Although they do not spread diseases or damage household furnishings, they often damage books and papers.

- **Also known as paper or dust lice**, they can be spotted in large numbers near stored books and papers in spring or summer.

- **These insects feed** on microscopic mould, fungi, dead insect fragments, pollen and other starchy food scraps and mildew that are found in a humid environment.

- **Book lice** run in a jerky, halting manner and sometimes appear to hop.

- **Their life cycle**, from egg to adult, takes from four weeks to two months or more, depending on the species and environmental conditions.

- **The outdoor species** of book lice are known as bark lice as they are found under tree bark or leaves. They feed on plant fibre. Bark lice are also found in birds' nests.

- **Bark lice live** in groups. They may be winged or wingless. The winged species, however, are weak fliers.

Earwig

🪰 **Earwigs belong** to the order Dermaptera, meaning 'skin wings'. They measure 25–30 mm and are flat and slender. Their colour ranges from red-brown to black. They have simple, biting mouthparts.

🪰 **These insects** usually have membranous hind wings, which lie hidden under their leathery forewings. Some species of earwig are wingless.

🪰 **The hind wings** open in a shape that resembles that of a human ear.

🪰 **Earwigs** have a pair of horned forceps, called cerci, at the tip of their abdomen. The cerci look like tails or pincers.

🪰 **Cerci help earwigs** to defend themselves. When alarmed, earwigs hold their cerci over their body much like a scorpion does. Although the cerci give earwigs a fierce look and can inflict sharp bites, they are quite harmless to humans.

🪰 **The male** has longer and more curved pincers than the female.

🪰 **Several species of earwig** release a foul-smelling liquid, which is produced in their abdominal glands. This helps to protect them from predators.

DID YOU KNOW?

One superstition is that earwigs crawl into the ears of people while they are asleep. This is how they got their name. Despite their threatening appearance and worrying name, earwigs are unlikely to come near a human, let alone crawl into their ears!

The female lays 25–30 eggs below the ground. She incubates them like a brooding hen. These eggs hatch into nymphs and gradually develop into adults.

Earwigs feed on algae, fungi, mosses, pollen, dead and live insects, spiders and mites. They damage flowers, vegetables and fruits by feeding on them.

▼ Earwigs are nocturnal insects. They live in the soil and can dig tunnels as deep as 1.8 m under the ground in order to escape cold weather.

Silverfish

Silverfish are primitive insects that belong to the order Thysanura.

These insects are soft-bodied and do not have wings. Silverfish have a longish body with three tail filaments.

▼ Silverfish are named after the tiny, shiny scales that cover their carrot-shaped body. They belong to a group of insects called bristletails because their abdomen ends in a central tail, which is fringed with bristles.

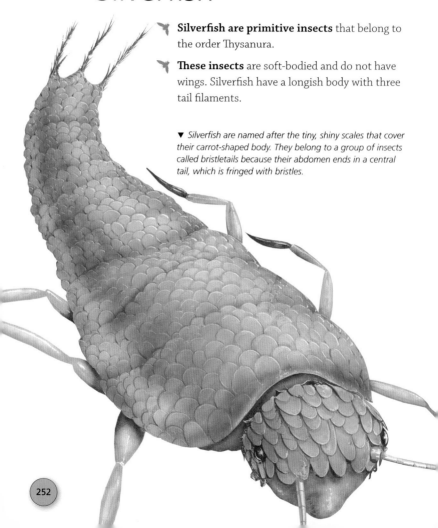

- **Silver or brown** in colour, silverfish can move very swiftly.

- **Silverfish prefer to live in** places that are dark and very humid. They are mostly found in moist and warm places, such as kitchens and baths.

DID YOU KNOW?
Silverfish are able to squeeze their flattened bodies into the smallest of gaps.

- **These insects generally feed** on flour, glue, paper, leftover food and even clothes. Silverfish can easily survive for months without any food.

- **Silverfish mate** in a unique manner. A male spins a silk thread and deposits his sperm on it. The female then comes near this thread, picks up the sperm and uses it to fertilize her eggs.

- **A female silverfish** can lay up to 100 eggs in her lifetime. After mating, she deposits clusters of her eggs in cracks or crevices.

- **Even after** maturing into adults, these insects continue to moult. They can live for two to eight years.

- **Generally harmless** to humans, silverfish can contaminate food.

- **Silverfish can destroy** books and are considered indoor pests.

Springtail

🌾 **Springtails** belong to the the order Collembola.

🌾 **Wingless insects**, springtails measure 1–5 mm in length. Unlike most other insects, springtails do not have compound eyes.

🌾 **These insects** have a springlike organ, known as a furcula, under their abdomen. It helps them to leap high into the air.

🌾 **Springtails** do not have a respiratory system. They breathe through their cuticle (hard skin).

🌾 **Even though springtails can jump**, they normally crawl from one place to another.

🌾 **Springtails prefer** to live in soil and moist habitats. However they can survive almost anywhere in the world including Antarctica and Arctic regions.

◄ *A springtail's forked tail is held under tension below the body, When released, it pings down and back, to fling the springtail away from danger.*

🪶 **Decaying vegetable matter**, pollen, algae and other plants are the preferred food of springtails.

🪶 **A female springtail** lays approximately 90–150 eggs in her lifetime.

🪶 **The lifespan** of a springtail is one year or less.

▲ *Springtails have to live in moist places because their bodies dry out easily. They are usually a grey or brown colour, sometimes with mottled colours for camouflage.*

Proturans

- **Proturans** are small hexapods (with six pairs of legs) measuring 0.5–2 mm in length. However, they do not have eyes, wings or antennae.

- **Proturans** belong to the order Protura and are primitive insects that live in soil.

- **Their abdomen** is divided into twelve segments, more than any other insect. They are the most primitive hexapods and some experts consider proturans to be very different from true insects.

- **Proturans** were first discovered in Italy but have since been found in Europe, India, the United States and Canada.

- **Fewer than** 118 species of proturans have been identified worldwide. It is the smallest class of Arthropoda.

- **Found in damp**, dark, moist places, proturans feed on decaying matter and other insects.

- **Proturans' mouthparts** are modified for piercing and sucking.

These **insects** have a unique tail, which is used for movement and defence. When threatened, they curve their tails over their heads and discharge a sticky secretion on their enemies.

Proturans use their first pair of legs as antennae.

▲ Proturans have neither eyes nor antennae. Instead, they have a sensory organ on their head and use their front two legs as antennae. Most species are microscopic.

257

Diplurans

Diplurans belong to the order Diplura. They are small insects and are usually less than 5 mm in length. However, some species can grow to 50 mm in length.

Although rarely spotted, diplurans are common arthropods and there are more than 200 species worldwide. They are related to proturans and springtails.

▼ Diplurans can be easily spotted in the wet forests of Australia. They are often found in small groups in the soil or under rocks or the bark of trees. Some species also live in ant and termite nests.

- **These insects** are blind. Their abdominal cerci look like pincers and they are often mistaken for earwigs.

- **In some species**, the cerci break off near the base if they are mishandled.

- **A tiny packet of sperm**, known as spermatophore, is deposited by the male. When a female comes across this, she fertilizes herself with it. This form of fertilization is known as external fertilization.

- **The female** lays her eggs in crevices, in the soil or on rotting vegetation. Some species are known to protect their eggs and young larvae.

- **Moulting continues** throughout their short lifespan of one year. An adult may moult up to 30 times.

- **Most species** feed on a variety of plant matter. Diplurans that have pincer-like cerci are carnivorous. They bury themselves in the soil with their tail on the surface. They wait for insects and capture them with their cerci.

- **Small vesicles** (sacs) on their abdominal segments help them to maintain the water balance in their body by absorbing moisture from the environment.

- **As diplurans** live in the soil and feed on plant tissues and decaying vegetation, they often damage plants by feeding on them.

Spiders, scorpions and mites

Arachnid anatomy

Arachnids include a variety of creatures, such as spiders, scorpions, ticks, mites, harvestmen and schizomids. Fossils of arachnids suggest that they were among the first land inhabitants of this planet. Arachnids can be found anywhere but they are most common in dry and tropical regions.

These creatures have eight legs. They also have two pairs of appendages (the chelicerae and the pedipalps) at the front of the body, which are used to grasp and hold prey.

Arachnids are classified as invertebrates – animals that do not have backbones. Instead of having lungs, arachnids have two types of breathing mechanism – book lungs and tracheae.

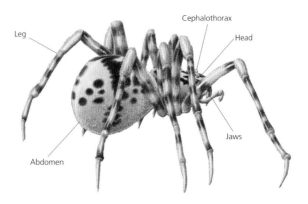

Cephalothorax

Leg

Head

Jaws

Abdomen

▲ Spiders are one of the best known archnids.
The abdomen of a spider contains silk glands.

▶ *An imperial scorpion. Although they are a widespread group of invertebrates, most arachnids are terrestrial (live on land). Scorpions are most commonly found in warm countries.*

Sting

Abdomen

Cephalothorax

Pedipalps (pincers)

Diverse in size, they can range from a few millimetres to more than 20 cm in length. They have a segmented body and a hard exoskeleton to protect them from enemies. The exoskeleton is a shell made of carbohydrates and calcium.

An arachnid's body is divided into two parts: the cephalothorax (joint head and thorax) and the abdomen. The cephalothorax has sensory organs, mouthparts, stomach and limbs, while the abdomen contains the heart, lungs, gut, reproductive organs and anus.

Arachnids do not have teeth and jaws to chew their food and most cannot digest food. This is why they suck fluids from their prey's body.

Sensory hairs, simple eyes and slit sensory organs are used to sense the surroundings.

Arachnids are cold-blooded creatures and get warmth from their environment.

Arachnids

🕷 **Arachnids are ecologically important** to humans as they help to control the populations of pest insects.

🕷 **The lifespan** of arachnids is fairly short. In temperate regions, they usually live for one year, but in warm places their lifespan can be longer.

🕷 **When arachnids walk**, they use the first and third legs on one side of their body and the second and fourth legs on the other side. These legs work in tandem to help them move.

🕷 **Certain species** attach themselves to the legs of other moving animals in order to move around. This mode of movement is called phoresy.

🕷 **Some mites** travel from one place to another by floating on the wind.

🕷 **Baby spiders** move from one place to another using a silken strand released from their body. The wind then carries this thread and the spiders hang on for a free ride. This technique is called ballooning.

🕷 **Ticks** are the most dangerous parasites of humans. Their main diet is the blood of mammals, reptiles and birds.

🕷 **Some species** of tick use their saliva to stick to living things so that they can suck blood. Once a tick is attached, it is very difficult to remove.

🕷 **When caught** by predators, some arachnids drop their captured limbs in order to escape.

Arachnids are feared by humans because of the painful stings of scorpions, the venomous bites of some spiders and the diseases caused and spread by mites and ticks.

▼ *A microscopic tick. There are estimated to be about 75,000 species of arachnid and these include scorpions, spiders, ticks and mites.*

Spiders

Spiders, along with scorpions, ticks and mites, belong to the family Aranaea within the class Arachnida. They differ from insects by having eight legs.

Found everywhere in the world, except in very cold places, such as Antarctica, spiders can survive in dry as well as moist areas.

Males are smaller than females. They may also have different markings or colouring.

▼ *The Australian redback spider is one of the most deadly of a group called widow spiders. These spiders get their name because once they have mated, the female eats the male.*

DID YOU KNOW?
The fear of spiders is called arachnophobia.

🔻 **When the male** finds the right partner, he usually mates with her immediately. However, some species secrete pheromones (chemical signals) to attract a mate. These spiders also have elaborate mating rituals.

🔻 **Some females** eat the male after mating. The male is often too weak to defend itself from this attack.

🔻 **The female** lays her eggs inside egg sacs made of silk threads. Each sac may contain hundreds of spider eggs. The sacs are either carried around by the mother spider or hidden in her web.

🔻 **Spider eggs** take a few weeks to hatch. Small spiders come out of the eggs. These are known as spiderlings. Young spiders may live in a group until they mature but some spiderlings live alone.

🔻 **Spiderlings** moult a couple of times before becoming fully grown adults.

🔻 **Most species** are solitary and only come together to mate. Some spiders, however, live as a community in which a group of females share one web.

▶ Spiders are predatory creatures. About half of the 40,000 known spiders weave webs or nets to catch prey. They can sense the vibrations when an insect rests on the web.

More spiders

Experts have found spider fossils that are 380 million years old.

Spiders are carnivores. They feed on all types of insect. Some bigger species can even attack small mammals and birds.

Most spiders inject paralyzing venom into their trapped prey. The prey is partly digested by this venom, then the spider sucks out its fluids.

Some spiders are very good hunters. They go in search of insects or wait and make a surprise attack on them.

Moth pheromones are secreted by some spiders. These chemicals attract male moths, which are fooled into thinking that the spider is a female moth waiting to mate. The spider then kills and eats the moth.

Many spiders are well camouflaged by their colours and patterns. This, along with their jumping skills, helps spiders to protect themselves from enemies.

Spider wasps are one of the main predators of spiders. However, scorpions, centipedes, small mammals and birds are also enemies.

DID YOU KNOW?
Out of the 35,000 different kinds of spider, only about 30 are dangerous to people.

Spiders are important to the environment. They are good pest controllers. Useful to humans, spiders prey on the pests that attack rice fields and cotton, apple and banana plantations.

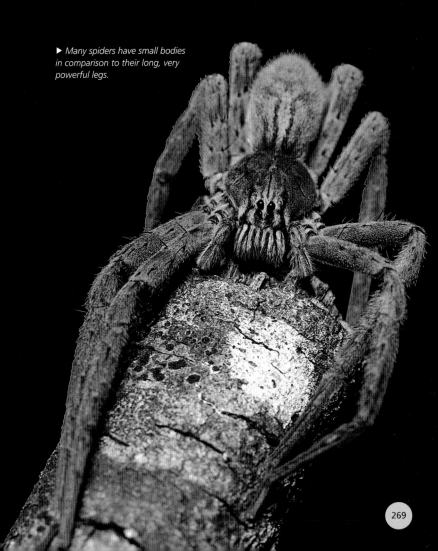

▶ Many spiders have small bodies in comparison to their long, very powerful legs.

Spider stories

The **scientific** name for spiders as a group is arachnids. This term is derived from an ancient legend about a beautiful Greek lady called Arachne.

Arachne was very talented and could weave beautiful patterns on cloth. Her work was so good that she challenged the Greek goddess Athene to compete with her.

Athene accepted the challenge but Arachne wove a much better pattern than Athene and won the competition. The goddess was very angry and tore Arachne's work into pieces. Arachne was so sad that she tried to hang herself. The goddess then felt sorry for Arachne and changed her into a spider so that she could continue weaving her beautiful patterns in the form of webs.

◀ Some of the best known spider stories come from West Africa and the Caribbean. They describe the adventures of Anansi, a clever, cunning spider – and are an encouragement to children to be clever.

Native Americans believed that Spider Woman was the creator of the Universe as we see it today. She made the skies, the Sun and the Moon. Spider Woman was also seen as the mother of all wisdom.

During the medieval period, Europeans believed that spiders caused madness and mass hysteria. They thought that people who were bitten by spiders would suffer from pain and laugh or cry for no reason.

Medieval Europeans also believed that music and dancing was the only way to cure the affected people. They later found out that spider bites had nothing to do with madness.

King Robert the Bruce of Scotland fought many wars against England and lost all of them. He hid from his enemies inside a cave and felt hopeless.

Legend has it that the king was inspired by a spider to fight once more against England. This spider kept trying to weave a web and did not give up, in spite of failing many times. King Robert the Bruce went on to win the next war against England.

Prophet Muhammad, the founder of Islam, hid inside a cave away from his enemies. A spider spun a web across the cave's entrance and prevented enemies from spotting the prophet.

DID YOU KNOW?

West African mythology has a very famous character named Anansi the spider. There are many tales about Anansi and his adventures. In the stories, the spider is described as being very clever and bringing fire, food and water for human beings from heaven.

Defence strategies

🦟 **Spiders** prefer to live in secluded areas and avoid trouble. However, these arachnids can become aggressive if attacked.

🦟 **Special glands** in a spider's body produce venom. They use venom to protect themselves and to capture prey. One spider family (uloboridae) does not have venom glands.

🦟 **Venom glands** are located near the fangs on the spider's head. If attacked, spiders stand on their hind legs and raise their head to display the fangs.

🦟 **Some animals** can be killed with spider venom, while others are paralyzed. Spider venom can affect animals in two ways – it can be neurotoxic or necrotic.

🦟 **Neurotoxic venom** affects the entire nervous system of the animal. It can cause paralysis and pain in areas other than where the spider has bitten. Necrotic venom only affects the tissues where the spider bites. The skin in this area can form blisters or turn black.

🦟 **Apart from** using venom, spiders protect themselves with the help of camouflage. Some spiders resemble bird droppings, while others look like dried leaves. These spiders avoid being noticed by predators.

🦟 **Other spiders**, such as some crab spiders, can even change colour to suit their surroundings.

▶ *A female tarantula guarding her eggs. The eggs are surrounded by a shell, or cocoon, of silk. Tarantulas may look threatening but are in fact shy creatures with weak venom that is not strong enough to kill humans.*

Spiders are hairy creatures. The hair may help with defence. When they are threatened, tarantulas hurl tufts of barbed hairs at their attacker. This leads to skin irritation and pain.

Sometimes spiders pretend to be dead if they are attacked. Predators prefer to eat live prey and leave them alone.

Most spiders do not cause harm to people. However, the venom of brown recluse spiders, black widows and Brazilian wandering spiders can kill people.

Silk

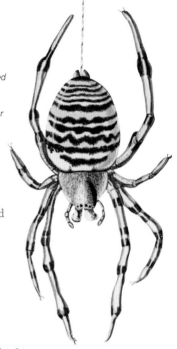

▶ White-backed garden spiders have distinctive silver, yellow and black striped markings. Like their close relatives, yellow garden spiders, they build large webs and often hang upside down near the centres.

Spiders specialize in secreting silk. They have special organs to produce silk. These organs, which are known as spinnerets, are located at the tip of the abdomen.

Spinnerets have lots of openings, called spigots, through which silk comes out. Each spigot secretes silk of a different thickness.

Spider silk is made of protein particles. Inside the spider's body, this silk is liquid in form.

The liquid silk hardens as the spider pulls it out to form a fine thread. Spider silk is very elastic and stretchy.

Many glands in a spider's body produce silk. Some spiders have seven silk glands. Different types of silk are used for different purposes. Sticky silk is used to capture prey, while non-sticky silk is used to make webs strong.

- **Silk is used** to wrap the prey, to travel long distances via ballooning and to make special sacs for spider eggs. Males also use silk to form a parcel of sperm.

- **Some spiders**, such as tarantulas, do not spin webs but they do line their burrows with silk.

- **Spiders** normally weave webs during the night and often finish making them by early morning.

- **Spider silk** has been used in a variety of optical devices, such as microscopes. Its strength and capacity to adapt to various climatic conditions makes spider silk suitable for such devices.

DID YOU KNOW?

To avoid getting stuck inside their own webs, spiders smear a special substance over their bodies and have oil glands on their feet. They only tiptoe while moving on the web. A spider also knows where it has laid the sticky and non-sticky silk threads.

Spools produce fine silk for wrapping prey

Spigots produce coarse silk for making webs

Several spinnerets produce silk

Webs

Spider webs are of different shapes and sizes. The webs can be grouped into three main shapes – sheet, orb and spatial. The most common are orb-shaped.

Spiders' silk is made from protein and it is stronger than a piece of steel of the same thickness.

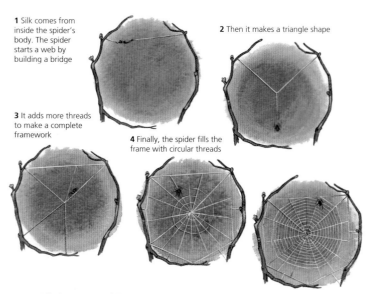

1 Silk comes from inside the spider's body. The spider starts a web by building a bridge

2 Then it makes a triangle shape

3 It adds more threads to make a complete framework

4 Finally, the spider fills the frame with circular threads

▲ *A spider begins its web by creating a strong framework of silk. It then fills the frame with sticky, circular threads that trap prey, such as flies.*

5 A spider's web is strong enough to catch large insects, but it is easily damaged by larger animals and people

Spiders depend on wind currents to lay the first thread of the web. They float the thread in the air and wait for it to stick to a plant stalk or some other support. Then the spider walks across the thread to continue weaving the web.

Orb webs are very light but they are made in such a way that the delicate web can support the spider as well as the struggling prey. This means that the web can handle a weight that is thousands of times heavier than itself.

Some spiders weave a web that resembles a hammock. The web is spun across two plants and the insect flies into it. The spider waits beneath the web for the prey to be caught and fall. Any holes made on the web are repaired later.

Sheet webs are also common among spiders. The spider weaves a sheet of sticky silk and lays it flat. Right above the sheet, it weaves a number of non-sticky silk threads. Insects that fly past the web will trip on the non-sticky threads and fall into the sheet below.

Not all spider webs are built against supporting structures. Some spiders use the web like a net. The net is thrown over the unsuspecting prey, which is then wrapped in silk.

DID YOU KNOW?
Certain spiders weave elegant webs and make special 'rooms' with doors, which they hide behind. They may also hide at a distance and only come into the web after an insect is trapped.

House spider

🕷 **House spiders** are the most common spiders. They are easily spotted in houses and gardens. They are also found in woodpiles and under logs.

🕷 **These spiders** have a yellowish-brown body with grey and black markings on their abdomen.

🕷 **Males are smaller** than females but have longer legs to help them walk long distances searching for females. The leg span of males can be as long as 60 mm.

🕷 **These spiders** feed on small invertebrates, such as beetles, cockroaches, earwigs and even earthworms.

🕷 **Sometimes house spiders** can survive without food for months.

🕷 **Webs are constructed** in the corners of rooms, under tables or chairs and in window frames.

🕷 **House spiders build** sheet-shaped webs and wait for prey to become trapped.

▶ Male house spiders may slide into the bath by accident while wandering around in search of a mate. House spiders are not dangerous but belong to the same family as black widow spiders, which are deadly.

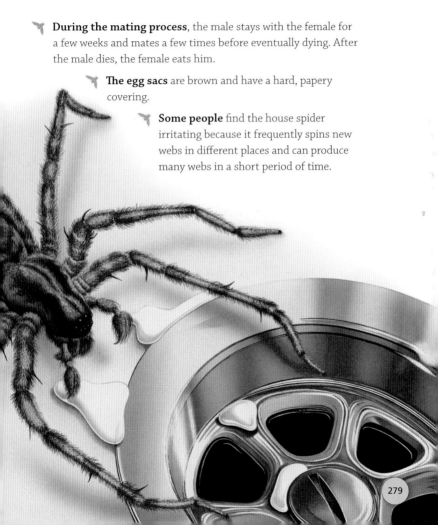

🦟 **During the mating process**, the male stays with the female for a few weeks and mates a few times before eventually dying. After the male dies, the female eats him.

🦟 **The egg sacs** are brown and have a hard, papery covering.

🦟 **Some people** find the house spider irritating because it frequently spins new webs in different places and can produce many webs in a short period of time.

Orb web spider

Orb web spiders are named after the orb-shaped webs they spin to trap their prey. These spiders are also called orb web weavers.

They are the largest web-weaving spiders. The webs vary greatly in size and structural design. Some species decorate the webs with extra silk.

Only the females weave webs. Most build a new web every night. They build their nests in open areas and between flower stems. It usually takes an hour to build a web.

A thin, sticky thread is released to start making the web. This thread is carried by the wind and when it sticks to something, the spider walks along the thread to make it thicker. This is repeated until a strong web is ready.

These spiders are found in a variety of sizes and colours. They usually have hairy bodies and legs. Their hair helps them to sense any activity around them.

Although most orb web spiders are blind or have very weak eyesight, they can distinguish between day and night.

There are many kinds of orb web spiders. Some of the most common are the golden orb web weaver, the St Andrew's cross spider and the cross or garden spider.

Male orb web spiders pluck strands of the web to attract the attention of the females. Females are usually larger than the males.

When prey is trapped in the web, the spider wraps it in a sticky, silky substance so that it does not tear the web apart. The wrapped prey is then either eaten immediately or stored and eaten later.

When disturbed, most orb web spiders fall to the ground in alarm. However, this is not true for all species. For instance, when a female St Andrew's cross spider is disturbed, she grasps her web and shakes it.

▲ *This fly is caught in the web of an orb web spider.*

Spitting spider

Spitting spiders belong to the family of six-eyed spiders, Haplogynae. They have six eyes and long, thin legs.

It is believed that spitting spiders originally came from the tropics. They are now found worldwide. In cooler climates they are most likely to be found inside buildings.

🦟 **These spiders** are shiny and have a light brown body with black spots and legs with black rings. They are quite small, ranging from 3–6 mm. Spitting spiders have a distinctive shape – a large dome-shaped head and chest area (cephalothorax).

🦟 **Found** all over the world, they live in dark corners of houses or around window frames and in cupboards. Sometimes they can be found outdoors under leaves and bark.

🦟 **Spitting spiders** usually hunt at night. They eat clothes moths and other pests.

🦟 **Little is known** about the mating habits of these spiders.

🦟 **After laying** her eggs, the female carries them around in her jaws. The eggs hatch about two weeks later.

🦟 **Spitting spiders** have a relatively long life span and live for two to four years.

🦟 **These spiders** are not harmful to human beings.

◄ *A spitting spider has silk glands, which are connected to its poison fangs. When it spots its prey, it spits a sticky silken substance over the prey to immobilize it.*

Funnel-web spider

Funnel-web spiders are medium-sized and have a glossy brown or black body. Their abdomen is usually dark plum or black in colour.

These spiders are named after their habit of making sheetlike webs that funnel into a tubular retreat at one point.

The spider hides in this retreat and rushes out when the web vibrates because prey has been trapped.

Moist and cool places are the preferred habitat of the funnel-web spider. It can be found under rocks and in crevices in wood or tree bark.

These spiders cannot jump or swim. The hair on their bodies helps them to trap air bubbles and stay underwater for a few hours.

The male follows a chemical scent produced by the female to find her burrow. While mating, the male takes care that the female does not bite him.

After mating, the female lays her eggs in a silken egg sac. The spiderlings emerge after approximately three weeks.

Spiderlings take about four years to mature but they leave their mother and fend for themselves after they have moulted twice.

The most deadly funnel-web spider is found in Australia and is called the Sydney funnel-web spider. The venom of the male is five times more poisonous than that of the female and a victim can die within 15 minutes.

▼ *Funnel-web spiders lay trip lines outside their burrows. These alert the spiders to any passing prey or mate and enables them to react quickly.*

Black widow spider

Female black widow spiders are one of the most feared and dangerous spiders. Only the females can deliver a fatal bite to humans. Males and young black widows are harmless.

Easy to recognize, females are black and have a red hourglass mark on their abdomen.

▼ *After mating, the female black widow sometimes eats the male, which is why she is called a 'widow'. She stores the sperm in her body so she can produce more eggs without mating again.*

Males are about half the size of females but their abdomen is more elongated and they have longer legs in proportion to their body. They have red and white markings on their abdomen.

Found in the warm and temperate regions of the world, such as the United States, Italy and South Africa, these spiders live in dark places such as drainpipes or under rocks and wood. They are not usually found in houses.

Black widows eat flies, moths and other small insects but their venom also works on vertebrates, such as mice. This might explain why their bite is lethal for humans since mice are mammals too.

Some female black widows live for more than three years; males only live one or two months.

Female black widows construct an irregular-shaped web, which is tangled. The core of the web is like a funnel and is designed to capture large insects.

Once prey is captured, the female wraps it in silk and kills it by injecting venom. The venom digests the prey and the spider is able to eat it easily.

The female lays her eggs in egg sacs, each containing several hundred eggs. She stays near her eggs and guards them. During this period, the female is more likely to bite if disturbed. At other times, when threatened, these spiders tend to escape rather than bite.

After about 20 days, the spiderlings tear the egg sacs and emerge. However, they tend to be cannibalistic and eat each other.

Brown recluse spider

Brown recluse spiders are small and brown. They are similar in appearance to violin spiders, which have violin-like patches on their body.

The brown recluse spider is named after its reclusive life spent away from others.

These spiders are approximately one centimetre long and weave a sheetlike web in dark, secluded corners of people's homes, under rocks or in forest areas.

Their small irregular webs can be seen in attics and cellars, as well as behind furniture and stacks of wood.

Long legs covered with tiny hairs give these spiders a velvety appearance.

Unlike most spiders, they have six eyes that are arranged in pairs over their head.

Brown recluse spiders are nocturnal and usually hunt for their food, mainly insects, at night.

Unaggressive creatures, they bite only when threatened by humans. Sometimes they can nest in unused shoes or clothing and if accidentally touched, they can bite.

DID YOU KNOW?
These spiders are highly venomous. A bite can cause irritation and even long-lasting sores. If people are allergic to the venom, the bite can be life-threatening.

- **The bite** of a brown recluse spider leaves a scar, which heals over a period of time.

- **Brown recluse spiders** can live up to ten years.

- **Males are smaller** than females. After mating, the females lay about 50 eggs.

▼ Female brown recluse spiders protect their eggs inside silk egg sacs. Spiderlings emerge from the sac in three to five weeks and moult six or seven times as they grow into adults.

Trapdoor spider

🐦 **Trapdoor spiders** belong to the order Araneae and measure 1.5–3 cm in length.

🐦 **These spiders** make burrows in the ground. They build a silk-hinged door at the opening of their burrows. The spiders wait for prey to pass and quickly come out of this door to grab a meal.

🐦 **Trapdoor spiders** feed on crickets, moths, beetles and grasshoppers. They generally live for up to 20 years.

▶ *Trapdoor spiders make the doors to their burrows using alternating layers of earth and silk. The top surface of the trapdoor may be disguised by a covering of gravel and sand.*

- **Some species** lay traps for their prey by stretching a silk 'trip-wire' from the burrow. As soon as a prey trips on the silk line, the spider rushes out and bites the victim. The venom kills the prey and also aids digestion.

DID YOU KNOW?
Trapdoor spiders are incredibly strong. They can move objects that weigh up to 140 times their own weight!

- **Trapdoor spiders** in the Ctenizidae families have a special row of 'teeth' on their mouth parts, which are adapted for digging.

- **Birds, centipedes, scorpions and wasps** prey on trapdoor spiders. Spider-hunting wasps flip open the trapdoor and paralyze the spider with their sting.

- **Some species** of trapdoor spider build burrows with side chambers and extra doors to help them escape from predators.

- **The female** usually spends her entire life inside the burrow and can mistake a male trapdoor spider for prey.

- **A male** is guided by pheromones (chemical scents) produced by the female and also by the pattern of silk around her burrow. Some males perform courtship dances to attract the females.

- **The eggs** are laid inside the burrow and are covered in a cocoon.

- **Not poisonous to humans**, the bite of a trapdoor spider may nevertheless cause some pain and swelling.

Mouse spider

- **Mouse spiders** are so-called due to their grey stomachs covered with hair, which looks like mouse fur. These spiders are sometimes mistaken for funnel-web spiders.

- **These spiders** belong to the trapdoor family of spiders. The two main species are the red-headed mouse spider and the eastern mouse spider.

- **Ranging in size** from 1–3 cm, these spiders have short, stocky legs and many tiny eyes spread across their head.

- **These spiders** can be found in all kinds of habitats, from deserts to rainforests.

- **Mouse spiders live** in oval burrows, which they dig in the ground. Hidden trapdoors cover these. After covering the walls of the burrows with digestive fluids and mud, the mouse spider lines the walls with silk.

- **Females spend** their entire life in the burrow but the males wander freely. Mouse spiders feed mainly on insects but they are also known to eat frogs, lizards, mice, small birds and other spiders.

- **Mouse spiders** do not spin webs to catch their prey. Instead, they usually hunt for them at night. Once caught, the victim is crushed and then immobilized with venom before the spider feeds.

- **Few males** escape alive after mating. The female lays about 60 eggs, which she wraps in a silk cocoon and places in a side-burrow halfway down her own burrow.

Once the spiderlings hatch, they continue to share the burrow with their mother. By doing this, many spiderlings are able to survive.

When they are in danger, male mouse spiders can be aggressive and usually rise up on their hind legs. They have large fangs, which can deliver painful and dangerous bites.

▲ A male red-headed mouse spider leaves its burrow. Females are smaller than males, and they are entirely black.

Tarantula

🐦 **Tarantulas** are hairy spiders found in the warm regions of the world, such as South America, southern parts of Asia and Africa.

🐦 **There are about** 800 different species of tarantulas.

◄ This massive, hairy, Goliath bird-eating spider has a 30-cm leg span. That's bigger than your head!

- **The hairs** on a tarantula's body are sensitive to touch, taste and vibrations in the air (sounds). The barbed hairs on the abdomen come off easily and can irritate human skin.

- **Tarantulas usually** dig underground burrows but some live in burrows dug by rodents or other animals. Some species live on the ground as well as in trees.

- **Tarantulas eat** a variety of animals from insects and small reptiles to small birds and frogs. This is why they are sometimes called bird-eating spiders.

- **Their powerful jaws** can be used to crush their prey. A tarantula's jaws bite straight downwards instead of moving sideways, like the jaws of most spiders.

- **Active at night**, tarantulas search for prey or wait outside their burrows for it to come near them. They kill their prey with their poisonous fangs. Then they inject a chemical to dissolve its flesh so that it is easy for them to eat.

- **Male tarantulas** search for a female by following the scent she produces. After performing the courtship dance, they mate. The female then lays eggs in her burrow and weaves a cocoon to protect them.

- **The lifespan** of these spiders is longer than that of other spiders. Females can live for up to 20 years but males do not live as long.

- **When cornered**, tarantulas purr and raise their front legs in a defensive position.

Hunting spiders

🕷 **Hunting spiders** include water spiders, wolf spiders, wandering spiders, nursery-web spiders, huntsman spiders and lynx spiders.

🕷 **Most species** do not construct webs to trap their prey.

🕷 **Some of these spiders**, however, construct large webs on the ground and run after insects that land in the web.

🕷 **Large eyes** enable hunting spiders to see their prey from a considerable distance. However, crab spiders, water spiders and tarantulas have small eyes.

🕷 **Hunting spiders** have strong chelicerae (a pair of 'jaws' used for clasping and killing the prey), which help them to hunt and capture their victims.

🕷 **The cephalothorax** (the fused head and thorax region) is usually larger in hunting spiders than in web-spinning spiders.

🕷 **Some hunting spiders** lie in wait for their prey and pounce on it. Others chase after their prey.

🕷 **These spiders have flattened bodies** and legs that point forward to enable them to slip under loose bark or stones quickly and easily.

🕷 **Vegetation and tree trunks** are the preferred habitats of hunting spiders.

Hunting spiders that do not weave webs, spin a silken thread and hang from it. They can use these threads to descend to the ground from high places.

▼ Hunting spiders such as this wolf spider have excellent eyesight, which they can rely on to find prey.

Crab spider

Crab spiders belong to the family Thomisidae of the order Araneae. There are about 2000 different species of crab spiders.

These spiders are named after their crablike shape and their ability to walk sideways or backwards. They are easy to identify as their first two pairs of legs are much longer than the rest.

Crab spiders have very small eyes. Although their eyesight is not very good, they can sense movement from almost 20 cm away.

🦟 **The female is larger** than the male and her body is almost round.

🦟 **Crab spiders do not spin webs**. They move slowly and are not good hunters.

🦟 **These spiders hide** themselves and lie in wait for their prey. As they can change their colour to match their environment, it is difficult for their prey to spot them. This helps them to make surprise attacks.

DID YOU KNOW?
Crab spiders are often found on flowers, which is why they are also known as flower spiders. They can change their colour to match that of the flower on which they rest.

🦟 **Some crab spiders** resemble tree bark, leaves or fruits, while others look like bird droppings.

🦟 **Many crab spiders** use venom to immobilize their prey. This helps them to kill insects much larger than themselves.

🦟 **Crab spiders** do not wrap their prey in silk after capturing and biting it. They remain with it until they have sucked it dry.

🦟 **These spiders prey** mainly on butterflies and bees that come to seek nectar from flowers.

◀ *The giant crab spider often hides, camouflaged, on flowers and attacks insects that come to feed there.*

Fishing spiders

🕷 **Raft spiders**, also called fishing spiders, belong to the order Araneae. They are dark brown with stripes on each side of their body.

🕷 **Males measure** 10–13 mm in length while females measure up to 22 mm.

🕷 **Raft spiders** live near water and do not spin webs. They feed on tadpoles, small frogs and insects.

🕷 **To locate its prey**, a raft spider lowers its front legs in to the water and feels the vibrations. The spider then pulls its prey out of the water and feeds on it.

🕷 **Raft spiders** can crawl down water plants if threatened and can remain underwater for 15–40 minutes or more.

🕷 **During courtship**, the male spider attracts the female by making regular waves on the surface of water. He jerks his abdomen up and down and waves his legs in the air.

🕷 **The female** is very aggressive towards the male and in some cases she might even eat the courting male.

🕷 **After mating**, the female lays more than 1000 eggs in a large egg sac.

🕷 **Green in colour**, the egg sac is carried around by the female. When the spiderlings are about to emerge, the female spins a protective silk web around the egg sac. She opens the egg sac and guards it until the spiderlings emerge.

▼ A raft spider waits patiently for the right time to strike. Its sensitive legs touch the water, feeling for any vibrations caused by possible prey, such as fish or frogs.

DID YOU KNOW?

The raft spider can walk on the water's surface without sinking. It spreads its legs out wide and takes quick, gentle steps.

Water spider

- **Water spiders** live in freshwater ponds, lakes and slow streams.

- **These spiders** are dark brown in colour. They have hair on their abdomen, which helps them to trap air bubbles and breathe underwater. This gives the spider a silvery appearance.

Water spiders construct a bell-shaped web under the water and fill it with air, which they trap in their hair. Once their retreat is ready, they stay inside and only leave to collect more air or to catch food.

These spiders can deliver a painful bite, which can cause irritation to humans.

Water spiders eat small fish and aquatic insects.

After mating, the female water spider lays her eggs in a white egg sac in her 'diving bell'. The spiderlings emerge in late spring or early summer.

While moulting, water spiders usually come out of the water to shed their old skin on vegetation near the pond.

The lifespan of a water spider is about two years.

These spiders hibernate in winter. In late autumn, the water spider seals its 'diving bell' and stays there all winter.

DID YOU KNOW?
Water spiders are good swimmers and, once they catch their prey, they clasp it with their venomous jaws and carry it back to their underwater retreat.

◀ Water spiders ferry air from above the water, down to their 'diving bells' that are anchored at the bed of a stream, river or pond.

Lynx spider

 Lynx spiders are named after their habit of pouncing on their prey like a lynx. They are very swift runners.

 Easily recognized by their narrow, conical abdomen, lynx spiders have spines on their body and long, thin legs. The cephalothorax is oval and the fangs are short. Males are smaller than females.

 These spiders are usually green in colour but sometimes they are orange-brown with yellowish green and silver stripes on their body. These colours help to camouflage them among vegetation.

 Lynx spiders have fairly good eyesight and their eight eyes are arranged in a hexagonal pattern.

 Commonly found on trees and in vegetation, they do not build webs, but wait on plants for insects and then pounce on them.

 Mainly active during the day, they can be seen running over vegetated areas and leaping swiftly from place to place.

 If disturbed, these spiders jump away. They seldom bite humans. However, when they do, the bite is painful.

 Females do not lay their eggs in webs. Instead, they attach them to plants. They are very protective of their eggs, which hatch after two weeks.

 One species of lynx spider, the green lynx spider, is considered very beneficial for agricultural pest management.

▶ *Lynx spiders are hunters, not web-builders, and they use speed, agility and good eyesight to seek and capture prey.*

Wolf spider

Wolf spiders belong to the order Araneae and the family Lycosidae. The meaning of *Lycosa* in Greek is 'wolf'.

These spiders measure up to 2.5 cm in length. They are usually found in North America, Europe, Asia and Australia.

Found in grass or under stones, logs or leaf litter, their habitats range from seashores to mountainous areas. Some wolf spiders can even skip across the surface of the water and duck under it for short periods.

These spiders are named after their wolflike habit of chasing and pouncing on their prey. They are also known as ground spiders or hunting spiders.

- **Most wolf spiders** are dark brown in colour and have a long, broad, hairy body with long, strong legs.

- **Ground dwellers**, wolf spiders are known for their very swift running speed.

- **These spiders have good eyesight**: the number and arrangement of their eyes helps scientists to identify them. They have two small- or medium-sized eyes in the top row, two very large eyes in the middle row and four small eyes in the lowest row.

- **Wolf spiders** use their front legs to grab prey, then bite to inject venom and crush their prey with powerful, jawlike mouthparts.

- **Courting wolf spiders** signal to potential mates by waving and drumming their palps (mouthparts) and legs.

- **The female** makes an egg sac of papery silk, which she usually carries around. The sac is shaped like a ball and is attached with strong silk to her spinnerets. After they hatch, the young spiders ride on their mother's back for several days.

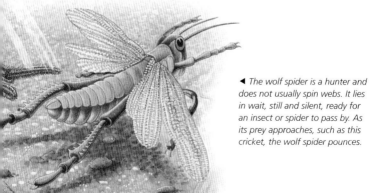

◀ The wolf spider is a hunter and does not usually spin webs. It lies in wait, still and silent, ready for an insect or spider to pass by. As its prey approaches, such as this cricket, the wolf spider pounces.

307

Jumping spiders

 Jumping spiders belong to the family Salticidae of the order Araneae. As their name suggests, they can leap across distances that are many times the length of their body. Hairy tufts on their feet help jumping spiders to grip surfaces.

Although mainly found in tropical regions, they can also be found in rainforests and on high mountains. These spiders love sunshine and retreat into their silken nests during cloudy or rainy days.

Jumping spiders are usually 1–2 cm in length. The female is generally larger than the male.

The spider jumps by means of muscular contractions in its body, which forces body fluids into the legs. This causes the legs to extend rapidly. Some species do not jump but scurry around in an antlike manner.

Many species of jumping spider are brightly coloured and patterned. They have stout bodies, short legs and large eyes on the front of the face.

▼ When jumping spiders leap they often produce a tough line of silk, called a dragline, which keeps them secure in case they fall or are blown off course.

▲ Most spiders have poor eyesight but a jumping spider's eyes form clear images of its prey. They can see clearly up to 30 cm away.

A jumping spider has much sharper vision than other animals of a similar size. It can see in colour.

Active predators, jumping spiders usually hunt during the day. They stalk prey and when they are close, they pounce.

Most jumping spiders feed on insects, while some feed primarily on web-building spiders. Some even feed on other jumping spiders.

The male's front pair of legs are coloured and have distinctive bands of hair. In many species, the male performs a complex courtship dance in which he moves his body and waves his front legs to attract a female.

After mating, the female lays her eggs in a silk-lined shelter under stones or bark, or on the surface of plants. The female often guards the eggs and the newly hatched spiderlings.

309

Daddy-long-legs spiders

▼ Daddy-long-legs spiders feed on insects and other spiders.

DID YOU KNOW?

When daddy-long-legs spiders are disturbed, they bounce up and down at great speed until they become a blur. This deters predators from attacking them.

🐝 **Daddy-long-legs** spiders belong to the family Pholcidae. They have a short, round cephalothorax with the head region elevated on the sides. The thorax region has a deep, long central groove.

🐝 **These creatures** are very small and have long, thin legs and a long, cylindrical abdomen.

🐝 **Daddy-long-legs** spiders are not very active and are usually found in residential areas, houses, buildings and even caves. They can often be seen in trees and under stones.

🐝 **The front eyes** are small. The other eyes are large and are arranged in groups on either side.

🐝 **These creatures** have venomous glands. However, they do not bite or harm humans. Their fangs are too small to cut or bite the skin.

🐝 **Daddy-long-legs** spiders feast on other spiders (including house spiders) and insects. They are natural enemies of the red-back spider.

🐝 **Sometimes**, daddy-long-legs spiders invade the nests of insects and eat the prey as well as their eggs.

🐝 **Their webs** are either sheetlike or irregular in shape. The daddy-long-legs spider hangs in an inverted position beneath the web.

🐝 **The female** carries her eggs in her jaws in a bundle until the spiderlings hatch.

Scorpions

🦂 **Some scorpions** can kill people with their deadly sting, but most have mild stings that are no more dangerous to people than a wasp sting.

🦂 **Scorpions sting** mainly in self-defence and to paralyze their prey. The venom is not usually poisonous enough to kill humans and other animals.

🦂 **Easily identified** by their venomous tail at the end of an elongated body, they also have four pairs of legs and two lobster-like claws (pincers) called pedipalps. The average size of a scorpion is 6 cm.

🦂 **Scorpions use their large pincers** as weapons to catch their prey, tear it into small pieces and crush it into a mushy pulp that can be sucked up by the mouth.

🦂 **These arachnids** can be tan, red, black or brown in colour. A hard exoskeleton protects the scorpion from external damage.

🦂 **Tiny sensory hairs** cover the body and legs and help scorpions to detect temperature changes and movement around them.

🦂 **Scorpions have book lungs**, which are structures for breathing similar to gills.

🦂 **Scorpions can store** a large amount of food inside their body. This allows them to live without food for up to a year.

🦂 **In extreme weather** conditions, the extra layer of fat under the scorpion's exoskeleton helps it to survive.

🦂 **At night**, scorpions use the stars to navigate and move around.

▼ Scorpions use their large pincers to grab prey, which may be bigger than themselves.

313

Scorpion life cycle

🐜 **Scorpions are nocturnal creatures**. Once it is dark, they come out of their nesting places, such as crevices, burrows or under rocks, to hunt for food or find a mate.

🐜 **Scorpions are known** to breed during the late spring, summer and early autumn.

🐜 **The male** locates a female by following chemical scents called pheromones.

🐜 **Mating is an elaborate ritual**. The male grabs the female and performs dancelike movements before mating.

🐜 **In some species**, the male is killed and eaten by the female once mating is over.

▼ The average lifespan of a scorpion is around three to five years but some species are known to live for as long as 25 years.

▲ *In some species of scorpion, the female carries the young on her back for about two weeks until they can fend for themselves.*

After mating, the female retains the eggs in her body and gives birth to live young.

Young scorpions are whitish and are surrounded by a membrane at the time of birth.

On average, a female produces 25–35 young at a time and she protects them until their first moult.

Young scorpions usually moult four to nine times before becoming adults.

Giant hairy scorpion

🐝 **Giant hairy scorpions** are among the largest scorpions in North America and have hair all over their bodies.

🐝 **These scorpions** have brown bodies and yellow legs and can be easily recognized.

🐝 **Although** they have very weak eyesight, the hairs on their bodies help them to detect ground and air vibrations and any other movement near them.

🐝 **Giant hairy scorpions** have a long tail, with a bulblike poison gland at the tip. They have large pincers called pedipalps to clasp their prey.

🐝 **Aggressive creatures**, they sting with the slightest provocation. Their sting is painful but not fatal.

🐝 **Giant hairy scorpions** are carnivores and feed on small insects and baby lizards.

🐝 **Mostly found** in desert regions, such as in California and Arizona in the United States, these scorpions can withstand extremely hot weather and are commonly found under rocks. They also burrow into the ground.

🐝 **Giant hairy scorpions** are nocturnal. During the day, they rest to avoid the heat. At night, they hunt for food or find a mate. They lie in wait to ambush their prey, then grab it with their pincers.

🪰 **These scorpions** maintain the moisture content in their body by sucking the fluids from their prey.

🪰 **Some people** keep giant hairy scorpions as pets. They feed them crickets.

▶ Also known as desert hairy scorpions, the giant hairy scorpion prefers dry, hot habitats. It can reach up to 15 cm in length and is able to hunt and catch prey larger than itself.

317

Whip scorpion

Whip scorpions are named after the long, whiplike tail at the end of the abdomen. Their first pair of legs is very long and thin and ends in antennae-like filaments, which are used as sensory feelers.

There are over 100 species of whip scorpion worldwide. The length of these scorpions varies from 25–70 mm. The largest species of whip scorpion is called *Mastigoproctus giganteus* and can measure up to 85 mm in length.

▼ Whip scorpions are arachnids, but they are not considered true scorpions. They are usually larger than scorpions and their whiplike tails do not contain stings.

Commonly found in tropical and subtropical areas, they usually live in burrows underground.

Whip scorpions have a flat body and can crawl into cracks and crevices. These scorpions can also be found under logs, rotting wood and rocks. They prefer to live in moist, dark places.

Quite harmless, whip scorpions have no venom glands and do not bite or sting.

These scorpions have glands situated near the rear of the abdomen. When disturbed, these glands secrete a spray, which is a combination of formic acid and acetic acid. This spray smells like vinegar because of the acetic acid, which is why whip scorpions are also called vinegarones.

Whip scorpions are carnivorous and feed on insects and worms. Some large species of whip scorpion also attack frogs.

While mating, the male transfers a sperm sac to the female. The female lays her eggs in a burrow and covers them with a slimy mucous membrane to stop them drying out.

After the eggs hatch, the young climb onto their mother's back and cling on with the help of special suckers. They moult three times in about three years before maturing into adults.

After the first moult, the young scorpions resemble the adults and leave the burrow. Soon afterwards, the mother scorpion dies.

Pseudoscorpion

Pseudoscorpions are not scorpions. They look like scorpions but do not have the long tail with the sting at the tip. There are more than 3300 different species of pseudoscorpions.

These tiny creatures range between 1–8 mm in length. Like scorpions, pseudoscorpions have two lobster-like pincers with which to grab their food.

Yellow or brown in colour, pseudoscorpions have oval bodies. They are popularly known as false scorpions or book scorpions.

Found almost everywhere, they live in woodlands, leaf litter, grass, birds' nests and anthills. They can also be found under rocks and on the bodies of insects and birds.

The pincers are usually small, reaching up to 3 mm in length. Many also contain a poison gland. This poison is used to paralyze their prey, such as springtails, mites, booklice and other tiny invertebrates.

Pseudoscorpions cannot chew. To digest food, they first pour digestive fluids (secreted by their mouthparts) on to their prey and then they suck up the liquid food.

Pseudoscorpions have silk glands, which have openings on the jaws, or chelicerae. They use the silk to spin cocoons, in which they moult and live in during winter.

The male performs an elaborate courtship dance before mating with the female.

After mating, the female carries the eggs around in a pouch attached to her abdomen. The eggs hatch into young and undergo two to three moults as they develop into adults. Adult pseudoscorpions live for two to three years.

▼ Pseudoscorpions produce venom in their pincer-like pedipalps, which they inject into their prey, such as this springtail.

> ## DID YOU KNOW?
> Pseudoscorpions often attach themselves to the legs of insects, such as house-flies, crane flies and beetles, to hitch rides. They can also walk backwards.

321

Horseshoe crab

Horseshoe crabs are the only marine arachnids in the world. They are also called king crabs.

Covered by a horseshoe-shaped shell, the cephalothorax consists of the head, neck and chest. The segmented stomach is covered by a protective shield. The rear end of this shield has a stiff, tapering tail, or telson.

▼ *A horseshoe crab's body is protected by its tough exoskeleton and its drab brown colour helps to camouflage it against sand and mud. Horseshoe crabs have two pairs of eyes.*

🦟 **Since this arachnid** has book gills for breathing and a shield studded with horns, naturalists mistakenly called it a king crab when it was first discovered. In reality, the king crab, or horseshoe crab, is related to spiders and scorpions, not crabs.

🦟 **The underside** of a horseshoe crab has a pair of small, pincer-like jaws and a mouth surrounded by five pairs of legs, which are used for walking and eating.

🦟 **Horseshoe crabs** are found along the coast of Asia and North America. They usually live on the seabed in moderately deep waters. In temperate countries they breed in spring and appear in shallow waters to lay their eggs.

🦟 **These marine arachnids are active** at night. During the day, they live partly buried in mud or sand.

🦟 **Horseshoe crabs feed on sea worms** and other sea creatures, which they find while burrowing. Worms and shellfish are broken into bits before being eaten.

🦟 **Females are larger** than the males and measure 50–55 cm in length. Although they look alarming, these arachnids are harmless to humans.

🦟 **Female horseshoe crabs** lay about 20,000 eggs in one night. When the young hatch out, they look like tiny adults, but do not have a tail. It takes them eight to ten years to develop into adults. Horseshoe crabs can live for 20 years or more.

🦟 **Like starfish**, horseshoe crabs can grow new legs to replace legs damaged by predators or the environment.

Ticks

Ticks are invertebrates that closely resemble their relatives, the mites, and belong to the same arachnid group as spiders and scorpions. They can be found all over the world. Around 850 species of tick are known to exist.

Parasitic, they feed on the blood of birds, some reptiles and mammals, such as humans, dogs and cows.

Ticks range between 2.5–11 mm in length after feeding. They prefer to live in temperate regions, in habitats such as grasslands.

These invertebrates have four pairs of clawed legs. They cannot run, fly or hop like other arachnids. However, they climb on grass and small plants, as well as on man-made structures, such as walls.

Ticks have strong sensory organs, which help them to sense the presence of a host so they can be ready to attack.

They climb onto the host and grasp with their legs. Immediately, they sink their mouthparts into the host's skin and start sucking its blood. When they have had enough food, they drop away from the host.

Mating occurs on the host's body itself. After mating, the female tick drops to the ground and lays her eggs. Male ticks usually die after mating.

There are two major groups of tick – hard and soft ticks. In a hard tick, there is a hard, plate-like shield covering the back and the mouth is visible from above.

Soft ticks have a spongy, wrinkled back and their mouthparts are hidden under their body. They mainly feed on the blood of birds.

The bite of a tick causes constant itching, which can persist for months. Ticks also transmit diseases to humans. The deer tick can transmit lyme disease, which causes fever, rashes and swollen joints.

▼ A tick is about the size of a rice grain. It has eight legs and is an arachnid, not an insect. When it has just gorged itself on blood, its baglike body swells up like a balloon.

Mites

- **Mites are oval-shaped creatures**, which belong to the order Acarina of the class Arachnida. They are found all over the world and around 50,000 species are known to exist.

- **Mites have an unsegmented body**, which means that the head, thorax and abdomen are fused together. It has four pairs of legs. However, in the larvae stage it has only three pairs of legs.

- **These insects** have adapted well to both land and water habitats.

- **Mites breathe through tracheae**. These are small, tubelike structures that open onto the surface of their body.

▶ These tiny creatures are so small that they may be invisible to the naked eye, but they are, nevertheless, an important group of arachnids. Some mites are free-living, others are parasites.

🦟 **Mites may live** freely in the soil or water but a large number are parasites of plants or animals.

🦟 **The most dangerous pests** for humans and livestock, such as cattle, they carry and transmit serious diseases.

DID YOU KNOW?

There are certain mites that live in mattresses and pillows, and are carried by dust particles. People use different insecticides and chemicals to try and get rid of them.

🦟 **Follicle mites** infect human hair roots. Bird mites harm the skin of birds. Chicken mites are known for spreading diseases in poultry.

🦟 **Scabies mites** attack horses, dogs and rabbits and cause itching and bleeding. Some Australian species can also inflict lethal bites.

🦟 **Mites can also live** on vegetation and plant fluids. They cause formations like galls on leaves. Some common plant mites are red spider mites. They spin a web on the undersides of leaves.

Red velvet mite

- **Red velvet mites** are soft-bodied. They are usually red or orange in colour and are 0.5–4 mm in length.

- **Their entire body** is covered with a fine coat of hair, making it look like velvet.

- **Red velvet mites** have four pairs of legs. Their front legs are used as organs to sense their surroundings.

- **The larvae** of red velvet mites are external parasites of insects such as locusts, crickets and grasshoppers. They feed on the blood of these insects and some cling to their wings, even in flight.

- **Adult red velvet mites** are predators of insect eggs, larvae and pupae and also feed on other small arthropods.

- **Red velvet mites** live in gardens, deserts and woodlands, where they are often found walking slowly over the forest floor.

- **After mating**, the female lays her eggs in the soil.

- **The eggs** hatch quickly and the larvae search for an insect host.

- **Once they have sucked** enough blood from their host, the larvae detach themselves and make a burrow in the soil, where they moult and emerge as adults.

- **Velvet mites** are becoming resistant to pesticides. Therefore, people are developing other ways to control them.

▼ Red velvet mites are eye-catching arachnids that live in woodlands and gardens. Their beautiful colour warns predators to seek food elsewhere as they taste particularly unpleasant.

Harvestmen

Harvestmen are often mistaken for spiders. They are not spiders, however, and belong to the order Opiliones.

Unlike spiders, harvestmen do not have spinnerets for secreting silk thread to make nests and webs.

▼ *Omnivorous insects, harvestmen feed on small insects, insect larvae, and spiders. Some are scavengers, feeding on dead creatures as well as animal dung and droppings.*

- **At first glance**, spiders and harvestmen appear similar. Whereas spiders have two distinct body parts, separated by a waist or stalk, harvestmen have a single, rounded or oval, body shape.

- **These insects are called harvestmen** because in Europe large numbers of them appear in autumn, which is the harvest season.

- **Harvestmen are usually found** in temperate regions of the northern hemisphere and Southeast Asia. About 6400 species of harvestmen are known to exist.

- **These insects can be spotted** living in hedges, parks, gardens or anywhere near vegetation. They usually gather in large numbers.

- **Usually 4–10 mm long**, harvestmen have fairly small, oval bodies. They usually have extremely long, thin legs. Many species do, however, have short, thick legs. Certain species are able to shed their legs when they need to escape from their enemies. In some species, the last segment of the leg has many joints, giving it extreme flexibility.

- **Harvestmen have two eyes** in the middle of their head. They appear to be looking sideways.

- **As nocturnal creatures**, they are most active at night. During the day, they hide away from the light by resting under hedgerows or in crevices.

- **Harvestmen are harmless** and do not have poison glands. They cannot sting.

Worms, millipedes and centipedes

Worms

Worms are long, soft-bodied animals without legs. There are probably more than one million different species of worms. They are an important link in many food chains, helping to maintain the ecological balance. However, they are sometimes harmful to other animals and the environment.

The worm world is divided into several groups. The three most important are roundworms, flatworms and segmented worms.

As cold-blooded creatures, they depend on the environment for maintaining their body temperature. Most species are parasitic, living inside or outside the bodies of other organisms and taking food from them. These other organisms are called their hosts.

Parasitic worms that affect humans are roundworms, tapeworms, whipworms, hookworms and pinworms.

Certain species of worm are free-living. They move around in the environment and forage for food. Worms can live in any kind of habitat.

In some species, the females emit a bright luminescence (glow) to attract the males for mating.

Aggressive behaviour is common in some species. They guard and defend their nests and tubes against other worms of the same species.

Some worms live in a symbiotic relationship with other organisms. A number of scale worms live in the mantle or the cavity covering of molluscs (shellfish) and starfish.

Marine worms filter food particles from the water and clean it up in the process. They are a type of filter-feeder.

It is difficult to preserve most worms because of their soft bodies and the absence of a skeleton. They are rarely found preserved as fossils.

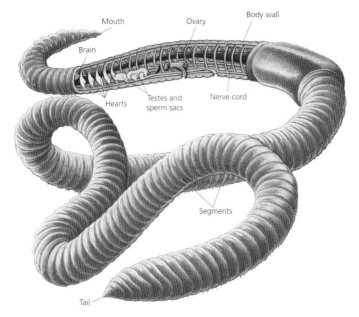

Mouth

Ovary

Body wall

Brain

Hearts

Testes and sperm sacs

Nerve cord

Segments

Tail

▲ An earthworm is a segmented worm, or annelid, because its body is divided into rings or segments. The word *anulus* means 'ring' in Latin. Tiny bristles on the segments help the earthworm to grip the soil as it burrows.

Roundworms

🪶 **Also called nematodes**, roundworms belong to the phylum Nematoda. These worms are found everywhere in the world. They can live on land as well as in water – both fresh water and salt water.

🪶 **Roundworms** have a round or cylindrical, tapering and threadlike body. It is not segmented. Most are less than 3 mm long.

🪶 **These worms** have a simple body structure and do not have a well-defined head.

🪶 **Roundworms** have a tubelike digestive system and a simple nervous system. They do not have a circulatory or respiratory system.

🪶 **There are many** types of roundworm, such as eelworms, hookworms, pinworms and whipworms.

🪶 **Roundworms have an outer body** covering called a cuticle. They usually moult about four times as they grow into adults.

◄ *Roundworms are among the most numerous animals. They can destroy farmers' crops.*

🐛 **The largest roundworms** are parasites of whales and grow up to 9 m long.

🐛 **In humans,** a roundworm infection can cause nausea, vomiting and diarrhoea. Doctors prescribe medicine to get rid of the disease. The best way to prevent infections is to eat well-prepared, clean food and take care of personal hygiene.

🐛 **A roundworm's eggs** hatch into larvae inside its host, which can be humans or other animals. These larvae are carried to the other parts of the body through the bloodstream.

> **DID YOU KNOW?**
> Roundworms cause dangerous, almost fatal, diseases in humans as well as in other animals. They usually enter the host's body through contaminated food, water, cuts or wounds.

337

Lugworm

Lugworms have a ringed or segmented body. The head and gills are dark red. The body is mostly thicker and lighter in colour than the head. It can be yellow, black-green or nearly black.

The body is thin at the tail end and the middle has bristles. Lugworms can have up to 13 pairs of feathery gills.

These creatures are found in estuaries and on beaches. Their presence is usually revealed by small holes in the sand.

Lugworms can be found in the sand within a U-shaped burrow. One end of the burrow is covered by a funnel-shaped hollow of sand or mud, while the other end is open.

▼ *Large numbers of lugworms live under the sand along the shoreline. The waste material they push out of their burrows piles up on the beach like squiggly heaps of 'sand spaghetti'.*

Lugworm burrows can be as deep as 60 cm. It takes about two to six minutes for them to burrow down, depending on the amount of water in the sand. The wetter the sand, the less time it takes.

When it wants to feed, the lugworm pumps water into its burrow. The water that flows through its gills contains sand. The worm digests the organic matter from the water and ejects the undigested sand in the form of casts on the surface.

▲ *Found deeper in the ground during the winter, lugworms live closer to the surface during the summer. They can stay in their burrow for eight months at a stretch and can survive for as long as one month in frozen sand.*

Lugworms are hermaphrodites. This means that the reproductive organs of both sexes are found in the same individual. The eggs of one lugworm are, however, fertilized by the sperm of another.

Lugworms play an important part in the ecology of the seashore. They are a major source of food for many fish and seabirds.

These worms are often used as bait by fishermen and are preyed on by flatfish and wading birds, such as curlews and godwits.

339

Bloodworm

Bloodworms are marine segmented worms, which belong to the Annelid group. They are mostly found on the eastern coast of America.

The length of a bloodworm can reach up to 37 cm. Their rate of growth is affected by the presence of food and the temperature and salinity (saltiness) of the surrounding water.

Bloodworms live in tubelike structures built on rocks underwater.

Excellent burrowers, they burrow into sandy mud or silty clay.

On their segments bloodworms have small fleshy projections or outgrowths called parapodia, which help them to move.

The parapodia also contain gills, which the worms use to exchange gases between their body fluids and the water surrounding them.

Bloodworms have strong jaws containing copper as well as poison glands, which they use to kill their prey. Their poisonous bite is painful to humans.

DID YOU KNOW?

To avoid overcrowding during the winter months, bloodworms redistribute themselves by swimming to another area.

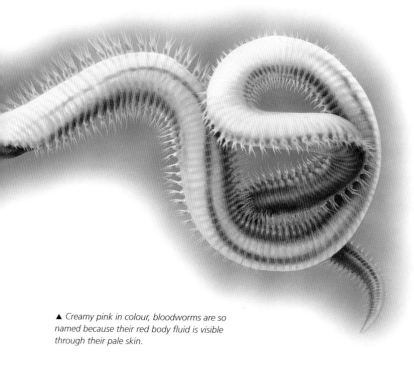

▲ *Creamy pink in colour, bloodworms are so named because their red body fluid is visible through their pale skin.*

Predators of bloodworms include other carnivorous worms as well as crustaceans, fish and seagulls.

After mating, the female releases her eggs into the water. Once the eggs are released, the female dies.

Leech

▼ There are around 650 species of leech and they belong to the same group of annelid worms as the common earthworm. Leeches have a sucker at each end of their body – one for feeding and one for hanging on while they feed.

✱ **Usually brown** or black in colour, leeches can range from 1–25 cm in length. They are known for their habit of sucking blood. In some cases, they can even cause death.

✱ **Leeches feed** on both dead and decaying plant matter. Some feed on insects and other worms, such as earthworms, while other species suck the blood of mammals.

Leeches suck blood by cutting through the skin with their sharp teeth. They fall away from a victim once they have sucked enough blood.

Living both on land and in water, leeches are found in mud pools, lakes and beneath rocks, leaves or logs. Aquatic leeches feed on the blood of fish and other sea creatures.

Leeches breathe through their skin. They do not have a digestive system. Instead, they have a pouchlike structure where food is stored.

These creatures lay their eggs in a cocoon, which they may deposit on land or in water.

Leeches that live on land wait for their victims in damp areas, such as rice fields. Once the victim approaches, the leech attaches itself to the victim's skin and sucks their blood.

With the help of their victim, leeches move from one place to another. They attach themselves to the legs or organs of the animals they feed on.

About 2500 years ago, the ancient Egyptians used leeches to treat all kinds of ailments. Leeches were used until the 1900s to drain the 'vapours and humours' believed to cause illness.

Today, some species of leech are still used to help skin grafts to heal, fight blood clots and restore normal blood flow during plastic surgery and reconstructive surgery. Leeches produce an anti-clotting substance that prevents clotting and keeps blood flowing freely while they feed.

Flatworm

🪶 **Flatworms are soft-bodied** worms, with flat, ribbon-shaped bodies.

🪶 **The three main types** are tapeworms, flukes and planarians. Tapeworms live in the intestines of animals. Flukes live in various parts of an animal's body. Both are parasitic. Planarians are non-parasitic, or free-living.

🪶 **Free-living flatworms** are found on land as well as in fresh water and salt water, while parasitic flatworms live inside their host.

🪶 **The outer surface** of free-living flatworms secretes a fluid, which forms a hard outer coating called a cuticle. They are covered with short hairs called cilia.

🪶 **Free-living flatworms** are coloured, while the parasitic ones are usually colourless.

🪶 **Parasitic flatworms** have a complicated life cycle. They may live in four or five hosts before they complete their life cycle.

🪶 **The reproductive system** of these creatures is complex and occupies a large area inside their bodies.

▲ Flatworms are the simplest of all the worm species. They do not have blood and a circulation system. Instead, oxygen and carbon dioxide pass directly through their skin.

All flatworms are hermaphrodites. This means that the male and female reproductive organs are found in the same individual but the eggs and the sperm are formed separately.

An interesting characteristic of flatworms is that they can reproduce asexually. They do this by separating into two halves to produce an entirely new worm. A new flatworm can also develop from a piece of worm that has been cut off.

Well-developed muscles enable these worms to change the shape of their body.

345

Giant tubeworm

- **Giant tubeworms** are found in the deep ocean near hydrothermal vents, which are hot springs on the ocean floor.

- **These worms grow** up to 3 m in length. They are firmly attached to the ocean floor and grow upright.

- **Giant tubeworms** live inside white tubes made of a hard, tough material called chitin. They have delicate red plumes, which contain blood rich in haemoglobin.

- **Giant tubeworms do not have eyes**, a mouth or a digestive system. At first, scientists found it difficult to explain the presence of blood and how tubeworms fed and survived in the dark ocean depths.

- **It was discovered** that giant tubeworms have a mouth and a digestive system in their early stage of development. Bacteria enter the tubeworms when they are young and remain trapped inside them.

- **It is the bacteria** that feed the giant tubeworms. The red plumes trap the oxygen and chemicals needed by the bacteria to manufacture food.

- **Chemosynthesis** is the process of making food without sunlight.

- **The haemoglobin** present in the blood of giant tubeworms collects all the chemicals that are needed by the bacteria. These haemoglobin molecules are 30 times larger than those found in humans. The blood carries the required chemicals to the bacteria, which convert them into food.

🦋 **The giant tubeworm** and the bacteria both benefit from their association. The bacteria are safe inside the worm, while the worm eats the food made by the bacteria. This sort of two-way relationship is known as symbiosis.

🦋 **Fish and crabs** bite the plumes of the giant tubeworm. For protection, the tubeworms quickly retract their colourful plumes into their thick white tube.

▼ *It was once believed that only microscopic animals existed in the ocean depths. It is now known that many life forms can survive in the absence of light and oxygen. Undersea vents give off clouds of hot water that contain minerals. These feed tiny plants and animals, which are eaten by tube worms in an early stage of their development.*

347

Pinworm

Pinworms are small, thin roundworms (nematodes). They are also known as threadworms and are common parasites of humans.

These worms are creamy white in colour. Pinworms have three lips on their head. They have pointed tails, which resemble pins.

▼ Pinworms are tiny nematode worms that mainly live in the last section of the host's gut, the large intestine or colon. They are a type of roundworm with longitudinal muscles (arranged lengthways) rather than circular muscles. This causes them to thrash and curl their bodies when they move around.

- **Females are much longer** than males. Males have a curved tail, unlike the pointed tail of the female worm.

- **Pinworm eggs** can end up on anything that a person with pinworms touches. They can live for about two weeks and are microscopic.

- **A pinworm egg** enters the digestive system. By the time it travels to the large intestine, the egg has grown into an adult worm.

- **The adult pinworm** attaches itself to the walls of the large intestine. It comes out of the human body to lay eggs at the anus.

- **Then the worm** travels back into the large intestine, while the eggs remain at the anus until they hatch.

- **The life cycle** of a pinworm may take one to two months. The affected person may not be aware of the infection until two months have passed by.

- **Children who are affected by pinworms** may lose their appetite. They do not feel sleepy at night and feel itchy. They may be restless in the daytime as well. Some people with pinworms may have no symptoms at all.

- **There are many medicines** available on the market to treat the infection caused by pinworms. The best way to avoid getting pinworms is to wash your hands before eating, after playing outside and after using the toilet. Keeping the fingernails short and clean is also a good idea.

Guinea worm

Also known as dragon worms, guinea worms are common parasites that live in the bodies of humans as well as other animals. The disease caused by this worm is known as dracunculiasis.

Guinea worms can be found in Asia, the Middle East, Arabia and northern and equatorial Africa.

Humans usually get dracunculiasis by drinking stagnant water that contains tiny water fleas, known as copepods, which are infected with guinea worm larvae.

This parasite has been associated with people from ancient times. Greek, Roman and Arabian scholars have mentioned these worms in their writings.

References to a 'fiery serpent', which caused havoc among the Israelites, may have been the guinea worm. It is also thought that the 'serpents' shown in medical symbols are actually these worms.

A female guinea worm can measure up to one metre in length and about 2 mm in diameter. The male is about 12–29 mm in length.

Females live for 10–14 months, while the males usually die after mating.

Both male and female guinea worms live in the connective tissue of various organs of the human body.

Females live just under the skin of the human host, usually in the legs, ankles or feet.

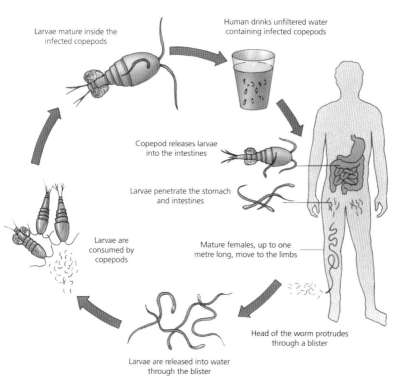

Larvae mature inside the infected copepods

Human drinks unfiltered water containing infected copepods

Copepod releases larvae into the intestines

Larvae penetrate the stomach and intestines

Larvae are consumed by copepods

Mature females, up to one metre long, move to the limbs

Head of the worm protrudes through a blister

Larvae are released into water through the blister

▲ The diagram above shows the life cycle of a guinea worm.

The developing embryos within the female cause her stomach walls to burst, releasing the young into the host's body. They can be found just below the host's skin. Eventually they emerge from a blister on the body of the host.

Earthworm

An earthworm's body is divided into ringlike segments. Most earthworms have a soft body. They are brown to red in colour.

Earthworms have five pairs of hearts. The brain, hearts and breathing organs are located in its first few segments.

Although they cannot see or hear, earthworms are sensitive to light and vibrations. Their mouth has a flap, which helps them to sense vibrations around them.

These worms feed on decaying organisms. They also consume large amounts of soil, sand and tiny pebbles. They ingest and discard food and soil equivalent to their own weight every day.

▼ Many animals, including the European mole, prey on earthworms.

DID YOU KNOW?
The giant Gippsland earthworm from Australia measures up to 4 m long.

▲ *The earthworm's burrowing activities let air into the soil and decompose organic matter, which helps plants to grow. The earthworm's waste material is also very useful in making the soil fertile.*

Earthworms are hermaphrodites, which means that each worm has both male and female reproductive organs. However, the sperm of one earthworm fertilizes the eggs of another earthworm.

While mating, two earthworms are bound together by sticky mucus and transfer their sperm to each other. The worms separate and form cocoons. Within a day after mating, the cocoon is deposited in the soil. Miniature earthworms usually emerge from the cocoon after two to four weeks.

Earthworms are known as clitellates. They are characterized by a clitellum, or thick band of skin, that produces the cocoon into which eggs are laid and also creates the sticky mucus that covers the worm and helps it to slide through the soil.

Usually found near the surface of the soil, they also make tunnels as deep as 2 m in winter.

353

Christmas tree worm

▲ *Christmas tree worms are a type of polychaete, or bristle worm. Their tentacles are intricate, delicate and often beautifully coloured, making them a favourite find of undersea divers and photographers.*

- **Christmas tree worms** are conical in shape and resemble a small Christmas tree.

- **These worms** are found on corals (colonies of tiny animals) in shallow seas. They can be many different colours – yellow, pink, white, blue, grey and sometimes brown.

- **Corals provide shelter** to many kinds of invertebrates (animals without a backbone), including the Christmas tree worm.

- **A Christmas tree worm** builds a tube on the surface of a coral. As the coral grows, the worm grows at the same rate to stay on the surface of the coral.

- **These worms** are excellent at sensing any movement. The worm lies in the tube so that only its head protrudes out of the end. If the worm senses danger, it immediately pulls its head down into its tube.

- **A Christmas tree worm** is covered in feathery gills that corkscrew around its body.

- **These worms feed on plankton**. The gills are covered in sticky mucus and catch tiny plankton, which float around with the ocean currents.

- **The gills** also allow the worm to breathe by exchanging oxygen and carbon dioxide with the water.

- **Many species of fish**, such as butterfly fish, feed on Christmas tree worms.

Myriapod

🪶 **Myriapoda means** 'many-footed' and some of the creatures that belong to this group have up to 400 pairs of legs. Myriapods are arthropods and their bodies are divided into segments. They measure up to 30 cm in length.

🪶 **Myriapods** are a little known group, although 11,000 species have been discovered. They are nocturnal creatures, which have not evolved much over the years.

▲ *A centipede. Centipedes and millipedes are the best known myriapods. Unlike insects, myriapods do not have a waterproof cuticle or skin and must remain in a humid habitat to avoid drying out.*

🪶 **There are four groups** of myriapods – Symphyla, Pauropoda, Chilopoda (true centipedes) and Diplopoda (millipedes).

🪶 **Found in soil**, leaf litter or under stones and wood, myriapods are difficult to spot. They prefer humid environments.

🪶 **Certain species** inflict painful bites on humans. The growth of myriapods is anamorphic – adding segments and legs with successive moults. Reproduction is usually by indirect sperm transfer.

🪶 **Myriapods primarily feed** on decaying vegetation. They break down dead vegetable material and play an important role in the ecological balance of forests. Some species are carnivorous and predatory.

🦅 **These creatures cannot migrate** and cannot survive in seawater.

🦅 **Many species** possess repugnatorial glands – glands that secrete foul-tasting chemicals that help to deter predators.

🦅 **Centipedes** have only one pair of legs per body segment and are predatory. Unlike centipedes, most millipedes feed on decaying vegetation, although some are carnivorous.

🦅 **It is believed that myriapods** may have been living on Earth as early as 400 million years ago.

▼ *Snake millipedes have shiny, cylinder-shaped bodies. They live in leaf litter and climb trees and fences to feed at night.*

Centipedes

- **Centipedes have a long**, segmented, wormlike body. Each segment except the last one has one pair of legs.

- **Centipedes are related** to millipedes. They differ from millipedes in having flattened bodies and only one pair of legs on each body segment (millipedes usually have two pairs of legs per segment).

- **These creatures** move very rapidly as they have 14–177 pairs of legs. They have one pair of long, many-jointed antennae.

- **Humid environments** are the preferred habitat of centipedes. They are nocturnal creatures and generally remain under stones, bark and leaf litter during the day. At night, they hunt and capture other small creatures.

🐦 **Centipedes are predatory**. The first pair of appendages on their trunk is modified into a pair of jawlike claws, which have poison glands. Centipedes use the poison to paralyze their prey.

🐦 **Centipedes prey** on red worms, insect larvae, newly hatched earthworms and various insects and spiders.

🐦 **Most species** of centipede are beneficial. However, the bite of large centipedes can cause humans some pain and discomfort, although there are no authenticated cases of adult human deaths caused by centipede bites.

🐦 **Besides poison**, some species of centipede secrete substances from glands found along their body segments. These secretions are usually non-toxic to humans.

🐦 **Not many fossil records** of centipedes have been found because they have a thin and light cuticle, which is not easily preserved.

◀ Centipedes are fierce predators. Their many legs make them swift runners.

Giant centipede

- **Giant centipedes** are so called because they can be as long as 30 cm. They have short, hooklike legs.

- **They are** found in tropical and sub-tropical regions, both in forests and deserts.

- **The colour** of a giant centipede depends on the area in which it lives. Giant centipedes found in rocky areas are grey in colour, while those found under the ground are almost black.

- **While some giant centipedes** are coloured to blend in with their surroundings, others display markings in vivid yellow and black. These colours alert potential predators to the poisonous nature of the centipede.

- **During the day**, these centipedes rest under stones, wood and debris.

- **At night**, they emerge to hunt for prey. These centipedes have a pair of long antennae, which helps them to sense the presence of any prey that are nearby.

- **Giant centipedes** feed on insects, scorpions and sometimes even animals such as small lizards, small birds and mice.

- **Giant centipedes paralyze** their prey by injecting it with poison and then crush it with their mandibles (mouthparts).

- **After the female** has laid her eggs, she wraps herself around them for protection. It usually takes about three weeks for the eggs to hatch.

- **Giant centipedes** can deliver a painful bite. However, they do not usually bite humans unless they are provoked.

▶ Centipedes are usually
found moving around
and chasing their prey in
a zigzag fashion.

Millipede

- **Although the word millipede** literally means 'thousand legs', millipedes do not have that many legs.

- **They belong** to the class Myriapoda and are closely related to centipedes. They differ from centipedes in that they lack venom and move more slowly.

- **Millipedes** have a segmented body, a hard exoskeleton and many jointed legs. Their body is a shaped like a tube.

- **Depending on the species**, they usually have between 45 and 400 pairs of legs.

- **Most body segments** have two pairs of legs. The first few segments, which have only one pair of legs, are called somites, while segments with two pairs of legs are called diplosomites.

▼ Approximately 10,000 species of millipede have been identified. These many-legged myriapods are similar to their centipede cousins in lifestyle and habitat, but they are slower-moving.

▶ *The rusty millipede is found in most places in the world and measures about 7 cm in length.*

🐦 **The penultimate segment** has no legs and the last segment – the anal segment – is used for excreting waste from the body.

🐦 **Millipedes** live in moist places on land, under rocks, leaf litter or logs. Some millipedes are garden pests.

🐦 **Spiracles**, which are holes found on their body, are used for breathing.

🐦 **Millipedes hatch from eggs**. When the young hatch, they have only the first three pairs of legs. Each time they moult, they add more segments and legs to their body.

🐦 **Most species** of millipede are herbivorous and feed on dead or decaying plant material. A few species are carnivorous.

🐦 **Birds and shrews** prey upon millipedes. When they are in danger, millipedes curl up in a spiral to protect their soft underside.

DID YOU KNOW?
When threatened millipedes can eject a foul-smelling chemical, which repels many predators.

363

Pill millipede

DID YOU KNOW?
Pill millipedes produce a squeaky sound by vibrating their legs.

- **Pill millipedes** are about 20–70 mm long and can be as thick as 30 mm. The species found in Asia are larger and thicker.

- **These creatures are shiny black** or chestnut brown in colour.

- **Pill millipedes** are nocturnal insects.

- **These millipedes** prefer to live in moist areas and are commonly found in evergreen forests. They are found in leaf litter and debris.

- **Although pill millipedes resemble woodlice,** woodlice have only seven pairs of legs, while pill millipedes have 17–19 pairs of legs.

◀ When disturbed, pill millipedes curl up into round balls to protect themselves.

▲ Like many other invertebrates, the pill millipede has a tough exoskeleton that provides both protection from predators and defence against drying out. Millipede exoskeletons are usually reinforced with calcium carbonate.

Herbivorous, pill millipedes feed on herbs, rotting leaves, moss and organic matter.

Female pill millipedes are longer than the males.

Females lay their eggs in holes and fill the holes with tiny pellets of mud.

The young emerge after two weeks looking like the adults, although they have fewer segments than adult millipedes.

365

Giant millipede

Giant millipedes belong to the order Spirostreptida. They are quite large and measure up to 30 cm in length. They have a segmented body and are either dark brown with golden lines on each segment or red with black lines. Each segment bears two pairs of legs.

These creatures are found in temperate and tropical regions of the world including deserts, caves, forests and along shorelines. Giant millipedes are abundant in tropical and arid coastal forests of eastern Africa.

Active at night, giant millipedes live in the soil or among plants. They feed on dead or decaying plant matter and have a lifespan of seven to ten years.

Giant millipedes have poor vision. Their antennae help them to find dead organic matter and decide whether it is decayed enough to eat.

The exoskeleton is made of calcium. Occasionally the centipede chews on stones or pebbles.

To defend themselves, giant millipedes curl up into a spiral. This helps the millipede to protect its head and soft underside.

DID YOU KNOW?

Young giant millipedes are abandoned after hatching. They grow and mature slowly over three to ten years.

▶ The Giant African millipede can grow up to 28 cm long.

Giant millipedes hide from predators beneath stones and plants. They can also produce a foul and irritating chemical from hidden glands.

The male attracts a female by moving along beside her and making her aware of the rhythmic pulses in his legs.

A female makes a small nest of compressed soil just below ground level. A few weeks after mating, she lays hundreds of eggs in this nest.

The eggs are covered with a tough, resistant coating to protect them from predators and adverse environmental conditions. The female guards the eggs until they hatch.

Index

Entries in **bold** refer
to main subject entries;
entries in *italics* refer
to illustrations.

Acknowledgements

All artwork from the Miles Kelly Artwork Bank

The publishers would like to thank the following sources for the use of their photographs:

Front cover Imagebroker, Adelheid Nothegger/FLPA

Back cover (t) David Benton/Shutterstock.com, (c) Anneka/Shutterstock.com, (b) Andrey Snegirev/Shutterstock.com

Fotolia.com 47 Marek Kosmar; 67 Patrick Bonner; 75 Seal do Mar; 87 schweitzer_aegen; 104 Cathy Keifer; 156 Wong Hock Weng; 166 dbvirago; 176 M.A.T.T; 210 Kakerlake; 238 FLYFISHERMAN; 240 Shocky; 242 FLYFISHERMAN; 305 Cathy Keifer; 310 Yann & Bernard Anceze; 313 noyiil; 342 WONG SZE FEI

FLPA 70 Fritz Polking; 78 JEF MEUL/FN/Minden

All other photographs are from:
Corel, digitalSTOCK, digitalvision, iStockphoto.com, John Foxx, PhotoAlto, PhotoDisc, PhotoEssentials, PhotoPro, Stockbyte

Every effort has been made to acknowledge the source and copyright holder of each picture. Miles Kelly Publishing apologizes for any unintentional errors or omissions.

MINI ENCYCLOPEDIA
BUGS

Mini book...
masses of knowledge.

Crammed with information on cicadas, butterflies, leafhoppers, diving beetles, termites, mayflies, spiders, earthworms, leafcutter ants, moths, assassin bugs, and much more.

- Detailed guide to the world of minibeasts
- Hundreds of illustrations and photographs
- Amazing fact panels

Miles Kelly

www.mileskelly.net

UK£9.99/US$12.95 RRP

Printed in China
Mfg date: April 2015
Batch number: ME715

ISBN 978-1-78209-445-6

9 781782 094456